# THE
# CHANGE
# GUIDEBOOK

# Praise for *The Change Guidebook*

"*The Change Guidebook* is an exceptional tool for creating positive change and adapting to life's challenges."
—former U.S. Senator **Olympia J. Snowe**

"If there was ever a book needed in our present times, *The Change Guidebook* is it. Elizabeth Hamilton-Guarino provides a concise guidebook for managing change for personal and professional development. Elizabeth will challenge you to think comprehensively while providing the resources necessary to help you effectively manage change."
—**Dr. Ivan Misner,** founder and chief visionary officer
BNI (Business Network International)

"We all aspire for growth, improvement, contentment—but we don't know where to start. *The Change Guidebook* not only helps us start, but it leads us by the hand and by the heart through the entire process of change. We emerge from Elizabeth Hamilton-Guarino's inspirational book renewed and recharged. We are different than we were, different and better. More whole, more self-confident, more resilient, and more of who we always hoped we'd become."
—**Dr. Harley Rotbart,** professor and Vice Chair Emeritus,
University of Colorado School of Medicine, author of
*No Regrets Living* and *Miracles We Have Seen*

"This guidebook is both transformational and transcendental. By providing the steps and tools to self-identify the problems, Elizabeth is offering herself as a fearless guide to an ultimate understanding and acceptance. Encouraging, delightful, important, and life-altering, this book uncovers who you are, and welcomes the person you're waiting to become."
—**Dr. Margaret Paul,** cocreator of Inner Bonding

"It is not an accident that you've picked up this book. You're ready for a change and this guidebook is filled with brilliant steps to help you along the way. It is jam-packed with great examples of brave individuals that have gone before you to have breakthroughs that will inspire you to be bold and ease into a new you."
—**Barbara Wainwright,** author, speaker, founder of
Wainwright Global Institute of Professional Coaching

"Change is challenging, especially when you didn't choose it. Support and guidance make the journey so much easier, and Elizabeth Hamilton-Guarino provides that and more! Elizabeth's excitement, experience, and enthusiasm in *The Change Guidebook* burst on every page. If you want to start changing now, *The Change Guidebook* will move you toward the introspection needed to get there. I highly recommend this excellent book full of life experiences of the author and other experts who have successfully navigated the waters of change."

—**Dr. Nancy Mramor,** award-winning author,
psychologist, media expert

"Allow Elizabeth Hamilton-Guarino to show you the way to make or adjust to change in your life. *The Change Guidebook* gives you everything at your fingertips to start today and create your best life. Change is up to you and this guidebook is the best place to start!"

—**Kris M. Fuller,** certified Master Coach and chief creative
officer of the Best Ever You Network

"This is a fabulous book to guide anyone who seeks a change in herself or himself to create a change for the better in their life. An effort must be made for that. The author offers a clear, step-by-step approach to guide anyone wanting to make such a change. Brilliant!"

—**Sally Huss,** author of *The Importance of Living Happy* and
100 children's books

"This book is the framework to help us craft a new way of moving through the world."

—**Sheri Salata,** former executive producer, *The Oprah Winfrey Show,*
author of *The Beautiful No: And Other Tales of Trial,
Transcendence and Transformation*

# THE
# CHANGE
# GUIDEBOOK

How to Align
Your Heart, Truths,
and Energy to
Find Success in All
Areas of Your Life

## Elizabeth Hamilton-Guarino

Foreword by Sheri Salata, author of *The Beautiful No*

Health Communications, Inc.
Boca Raton, Florida
*www.hcibooks.com*

**Other Books by Elizabeth Hamilton-Guarino**
PERCOLATE: *Let Your Best Self Filter Through*

**Books by Elizabeth Hamilton-Guarino and Kris M. Fuller**
*Pinky Doodle Bug*
*Pinky Doodle Dance*
*Best Ever You: 52-Week Journal to Your Bravest, Boldest You*

**Books by Elizabeth Hamilton-Guarino and Sally Huss**
*Best Ever You*
*A Lesson for Every Child: Learning About Food Allergies*
*Self-Confident Sandy*

**Library of Congress Cataloging-in-Publication Data**
**is available through the Library of Congress**

© 2022 Elizabeth Hamilton-Guarino

ISBN-13: 978-0-7573-2421-5  (Paperback)
ISBN-10: 0-7573-2421-5 (Paperback)
ISBN-13: 978-0-7573-2422-2 (ePub)
ISBN-10: 0-7573-2422-3  (ePub)

HCI, its logos, and marks are trademarks of Health Communications, Inc.

Publisher:  Health Communications, Inc.
            1700 NW 2nd Avenue
            Boca Raton, FL 33432-1653

*Cover design by Larissa Hise Henoch*
*Interior design by Larissa Hise Henoch, formatting by Lawna Patterson Oldfield*

# DEDICATION

• • • •

*For real people who lead real lives and desire real change.*
*This book is for all who need to be met in that*
*moment to receive help finding their way.*
*Always remember, your positive energy fuels humanity.*
*For Peter, Connor, Quinn, Cam, and Quaid*
*For my parents: James and Carolyn Hamilton*
*For Kris M. Fuller in loving memory of Ben Fuller*

# CONTENTS

• • •

## I believe

*You must think with your heart.*

*Live and show up authentically.*

*Understand you go where you place your energy.*

*When these things align, you can do anything.*

**—Elizabeth Hamilton-Guarino**

# FOREWORD

● ● ●

**Forward** [sic], indeed.

For the first time, a more aligned moment—a more divine opportunity—has come to dive deep and discover what we genuinely want for our lives. We have access to education, international learning, cutting-edge technology, world-class coaches, networks, and more. We can figure out how we imagine our best ever selves.

But how do we do it?

That is the question that has confounded many of us who know we need a change, a transformation, an overhaul of the way we do life. We feel the need, the longing, the call, but we aren't sure where to even place our feet to take those first steps.

Enter *The Change Guidebook*.

This book offers the framework to help us craft a new way of moving through the world, a new way of inhabiting our lives, and a new experience of living life as someone firmly grounded in our values and expanded by a consistent, moment-by-moment practice of gratitude.

But what are our values? When was the last time we gave ourselves the space to determine what we value? Now, with all we have experienced in life, what is most important? Without knowing what we value and focusing on those values, our lives run us. We find ourselves tossed and turned by external events, always reacting—never holding the reins entirely in our own hands. And deep inside, we know that unstable and insecure are not the way we really want to live.

We want to be happy more than we are unhappy.

A bottom line eventually must be faced if we are truly ready to level up our experience: right here, right now. If we want to squeeze all the juice out of this trip on Earth, we must mindfully run our own lives. No one else can do it for us.

Let's begin with a beautiful examination of where we are right now. Ask ourselves the crucial questions: *What do we keep? What do we amplify and expand? What do we change?* This book guides us to answer all these questions.

What Elizabeth has created is an awe-inspiring offering of vulnerability as she shares herself, her stories, and the wisdom she and others have acquired on their respective journeys. Wisdom that can help light our own paths.

This is the moment to go inward to go forward.

Here is your plan.

—**Sheri Salata,** author of *The Beautiful No*

# ACKNOWLEDGMENTS

• • •

**While writing a book,** there is a support crew that rubs your weary fingers, hands, and back and listens to your varying degrees of great and no-so-great ideas, for they are your trusted crew. In this case my husband, Peter, and our four sons, Connor, Quinn, Cam, and Quaid, win my very made-up award for Best Book Writing Support Team. You are a constant source of love and encouragement. You all amaze me with your own joy and successes, as well as love and kindness to those in the world around you.

Speaking of sources of love, my huge family in Minnesota, New Jersey, New York, and Iowa is an amazing built-in book and fan club. My dad would have loved to have seen this moment, although I do believe he is always with me. My mom is so proud, and her love guides our family. Thank you always. There is a moment in the car with my mom that was pivotal as I listened to her for a few hours while it rained. The life lessons shared guided me to this moment.

And then there are the friends who are family. Sheri Salata and Kris M. Fuller are both guiding lights. You can chart a guiding course to their stars that shine so brilliantly in the Universe. I'm forever grateful for your belief in me and your love, confidence, support, kindness, and brilliance. I could fill a book with how these two women have changed my life, so expect those stories woven into this book.

To our entire Best Ever You Network, this also would not be possible without you. It takes a huge team to help an author shout to the world, "My new book has been released and it is awesome! Please read it, learn from it, and share it." And that is what you all help me do.

Thank you to those friends who viewed and edited this in real time and provided valuable feedback and edits. Thank you to Jennifer Vaughn for challenging me. Thank you to Barbara Wainwright for lighting up the runway. Very special thanks also to Sherianna Boyle, Denise Zack, Dr. Margaret Paul, Dr. Lynne Celli, and Dr. Nancy Mramor for their expert guidance, suggestions, and support.

As I was writing this and reflecting on some of my own experiences as a child and young adult, which was mostly a grand life, I look back and often think of those I went to school with, those who put on a happy face, and you never knew what was going on in their life for real unless you looked much closer. Here in Maine, this makes me think about the Olympia Snowe Leadership Institute for Women. The work Senator Olympia J. Snowe has championed has brought me to tears many times. I'm proud to say I have been a Leadership Advisor for several years now and am extremely honored to present Senator Olympia J. Snowe's story in this book in Chapter 10. Thank you, Senator Olympia J. Snowe, for inspiring women of all ages and for your incredible commitment to others and helping us all find success in all areas of our lives when finding our values, voice, and vision.

Thank you to Steve Harris who helped me find my footing and gave me direction again. I'm forever grateful. It is a privilege to have faced rejection and joy with you, often on the same day or even hour. Also, a very special thank-you to Amy Scher, who selflessly contributed her expertise to help me be my best. Thank you again. You are a guide to many in this industry, and I'm grateful for your love and support.

My journey with Steve brought us to HCI. Christine Belleris, Christian Blonshine, Lindsey Mach, Camilla Michael, Allison Janse, and Larissa Henoch were all in, from day one. Thank you for your expertise and kindness. A very special thank-you also to Dr. Harley Rotbart, author of *No Regrets Living,* for getting me unstuck and helping me in multiple ways with this book. That selfless moment and the ones that followed have helped me so much. I absolutely love it when an author is as wonderful in person and in real life as they appear to be in their book. Thank you for your incredible smile, humor, and wisdom.

My gratitude to the following for sharing their stories with us: Barbara Wainwright, Omar Kingston, Quaid Guarino, Brian J. Esposito, Dr. Harley Rotbart, Denise Zack, Paul, Fiona Joy Hawkins, Kris M. Fuller, Deb Landry, Lisa Sedgwick Minakowski, Gary Kobat, E. J. Yerzak, Dave Strauss, Brian Hilliard, Eleanor Garrow-Holding, Sarah Cronk, Dr. Ivan Misner, Sally Huss, Haley Stark, and Senator Olympia J. Snowe. I'm so honored to know you all and see all you do in this world to make a difference.

Love, Elizabeth

# INTRODUCTION

● ● ●

**Can you imagine** if our calls at the Best Ever You Network sounded like this? "Hi, Elizabeth. I'd like to be miserable at my job, say at least 30,000 negative comments a day to myself, start smoking, drink heavily, be as broke as possible, never be good at anything, and spend all my hours in life mastering the path to complete failure."

As a certified master coach and change facilitator, I'm so glad my days and calls actually go more like, "I'd like to be happier, can you help me?" and so on. Most of the clients I help are well-intentioned people who want to change something in their lives: They want to eat as best as they can, talk positively to themselves, be a better partner, or master a path to more joy. I've guided people across the globe to find success in all areas of their lives with the process you will learn in this book. Whether it's professional success you seek or the skills to resolve an unforeseen event, my purpose is to guide you to feel and be your best.

While we all seek to be the best we can, it's common and expected that we'll struggle at times. If you're struggling with change, it means you're exactly where you need to be, right here with me, as I help you overcome the obstacles in your way. We're in constant need of alignment: When things align, the shift can begin. *True change happens when you align your heart, your truths, and your energy.*

The extreme demands of our world challenge alignment. From time management to the choices we make and actions we take or don't take, we

1

are often derailed from our goals or unable to cope with the changes that life brings. This book breaks down attainable goals and behaviors into bite-sized opportunities for change. The process is based on the Ten Points of Change, a process of recognizing, allowing, and committing to actionable, sustainable change in your life.

I'll guide you to find perspective—a perspective so great that you take the time to align everything about yourself: to who you are at your core and what matters the most. I passionately believe that nearly everything revolves around our ability to manage our time and how we make or deal with change. Our attitude in how we approach each moment provides the insight to cherish them all with gratitude, no matter the happenings.

Picture your life as a series of breathtaking moments in which you have strong feelings of confidence, worth, success, and peace. All areas of life are in alignment. You have momentum and positive energy. If your life isn't like this, it can be, and while each moment of your life matters, I can help you find a new perspective.

Remember, you have a choice in every moment of how to be. You have choices in what you say, what you do, how you react, and more—so many opportunities to choose in each moment every day.

This is an invitation to learn, accept, and apply the Ten Points of Change to a new life approach that is well worth the investment. This process doesn't happen quickly. Change takes time, commitment, and discipline, but it is worth the investment. Investing in the best ever you.

Before we get started, please know that this book is really from my heart, truths, and energy to yours. I'll be sharing stories about my life and obstacles, victories, and more along the way. I'm right here for you. I believe we need one another. One huge component of success is teamwork, even if it appears to be or has been a solo adventure or success story. So, if you have questions as you go through this process, please reach out to me. I am genuinely fascinated with people and would love to learn more about you. I believe it is important to touch each life we encounter with grace, elegance, compassion, and a keen sense of collaboration in an effort to connect the dots to help one another.

## How to Use *The Change Guidebook*

This book is straightforward, divided into three focus areas with ten chapters total. Each of the ten chapters represents a point of change. Each chapter is followed by two exercises and some other prompts for your writing. Think of these as true practice areas to put in motion what you learned.

I've also woven in stories of real people, real action, and real change from members of our Best Ever You Network. I love a great success story. In each chapter, we are going to share a tale of excellence from our Best Ever You Network—a moment where the ordinary feels extraordinary and the brilliance of the achievement sparks a light within each of us to keep going. That feeling connects us and gives us the faith or hope we need to carry on, charge forward, and even double down in a moment when we previously felt like giving up.

If you are one of those people like me who doesn't like writing in an actual printed book, keep a journal or notebook dedicated to your journey. In addition, all exercises are available for download. Also, at the end of each part, you have an option to submit your work to ultimately receive a certificate upon the completion of the book: *The Change Guidebook* master class certificate. More information is available at besteveryou.com/changeguidebook.

## The Ten Points of Change

Change takes time, commitment, discipline, and alignment. We change with every new influence that enters our life.

Align Your **HEART**

Align Your **TRUTHS**

Align Your **ENERGY**

**POINT 1**
ASSESS

**POINT 5**
SUPPORT

**POINT 8**
ENGAGE

**POINT 2**
CHOOSE

**POINT 6**
IMPLEMENT

**POINT 9**
MASTER

**POINT 3**
DISCOVER

**POINT 7**
ACCEPT

**POINT 10**
IMPACT

**POINT 4**
GROW

These are the Ten Points of Change I developed years ago when I started the Best Ever You Network. These ten points help my clients create lasting change, make incredible improvements in their lives, or cope with unforeseen changes. Whether you need to adjust to circumstances and change or you want to take control of the reins, this process can be used time and time again to rebalance and adjust.

My goal is to help you master the Ten Points of Change, so that you have the tools to work through a process when faced with something you want to improve, stop, or change. These points can help you navigate any hurdle or situation you face on the journey to becoming your best.

Commit to live differently. Commit to be your best. You only get one passage, one ticket on the train of life. Many stops occur along the way, forks in the road, choices at every turn. Are you on the path you want to be in every area of your life?

Decide that today is your Day 1. This is the first step forward, when you listen to that inkling that your best life is just ahead. This book is the key resource in your toolbox of life to build your best life and be your best you.

# PART 1

# ALIGN YOUR HEART

# CHAPTER 1
# ASSESS

*In this first point, we practice self-awareness and self-reflection. We examine the truth and what you want to change and where you want your life to go. If you don't know about it, you can't change it, so this point entails honest, authentic self-reflection.*

**Think of yourself as a collector of data** and the information is all about you. Who you are, what you do, why you do what you do, where you are in life, how you feel, and more. As you collect information voluntarily or involuntarily, your heart is a data processor. It examines the heart-based truth about what you want to change and where you want your life to go. This is a point of honest self-reflection to make change deliberately or adapt to an unforeseen change or unexpected circumstance.

In these situations, take inventory and assess the situation. Don't assess in comparison to others because that blocks gratitude. Remember, as someone is ticking, another is tocking; as someone is zigging, another is zagging.

Be authentically you. This is an honest assessment in all areas of your life, including the language you use with yourself and perhaps others.

Let's begin aligning your heart, truths, and energy to find success in all areas of your life. We will begin with one of the most important tips for success.

## SUCCESS TIP #1: Be Brave and Think with Your Heart

Your heart is your main operational center. So many people ignore their heart because they are overthinking. Too much brain-based thinking creates a situation where you lose sight of thinking with your heart. When you aren't tuned in to hear your heart, you get caught up in the cycle of overthinking. Please take a moment with me to pause and place your hands over your heart and say, "I am brave. I think with my heart." I do this pause practice and affirmation each morning and perhaps multiple times during the day.

## SUCCESS TIP #2: Know That Your Heart Is Your Authentic Guidance System

It's true. Trust your heart. Often we don't 100 percent trust our heart and instincts because we may feel that they've failed us before. This leads to us possibly ignoring our heart to protect ourselves. With this method we potentially miss so much. To align with your heart as you are going through this process, move from your head to your heart and think with your heart.

Multiple people who begin working with me produce elaborate decision charts, decision trees, and pros-and-cons lists. In some instances those work, but not in all. Some assessments are best answered and thought through with a heart-centered focus. Don't turn the volume down on what your heart says to you. How do you feel? What are you passionate about? If you are thinking, *Elizabeth, I am an executive who needs to think with my brain 24/7; I don't have room for all this heart-centered stuff,* I hear you and I'm going to challenge you and say the best dollar you will ever earn is the dollar you are most passionate about and perhaps the best dollar someone spends will be on you. It might even be a dollar you spend on yourself!

I completely understand the noise from people everywhere telling you about inner self-awareness, to listen to your gut/heart/soul, to let yourself soar in your new light and awareness—all that kind of stuff. Maybe people are saying this for a reason, for we all know when we are on the receiving end of less than warm feelings of another who isn't a heart-based thinker. Don't be that person who gets lost or leaves something in your life unfulfilled by missing that incredible connection to that base feeling.

We can be great at the accountability stuff—the checklists and all that we can measure with ease—however, when digging a little deeper at the construct of listening to our hearts, we must pay attention to more of what we actually *feel*.

For instance, a client said to me, "I was so worried. Every morning felt like a warning shot rather than a new beginning. My heart was bogged down with stress and fear. I felt like I was surviving a storm rather than meeting a goal. My head hurt, my arms felt heavy, my stomach rolled."

In this case, as he started to pay more attention to how he actually felt, he began to learn to recognize how to listen to those feelings and connect with them, and he understood that we can have actual physical and mental manifestations of all that we're working to overcome. Connect with a feeling. This becomes your reason to stay motivated and inspired.

Here is another instance, from a friend, Jamie. She said to me, "I was so overjoyed. I put on my jeans that I hadn't worn in seven years. It's been the most incredible feeling to not only weigh less but to also feel actually lighter in so many ways that aren't scale focused. I can dance with my husband. I can wear a bathing suit on the beach. Yes, I could have done those things before, but now that inner voice that always brought me down or talked me out of doing things is quieted."

I'm suggesting a full-on gut check and heart check! Listen for when your heart is talking to you. It barks at you louder than the dogs. It may even scream at you. It aches, it beats fast. Your heart has many responses. Your heart gives you hints. Your heart keeps you alive. Your heart's purpose is life, so aid it with living your best life. Your heart helps your gut and coordinates your inner voice and feeling so that you are able to feel and respond to your emotions.

The tricky part is, our heart assessments aren't entirely tangible either. It's easy to take an assessment of your bank account; you see the balance and the number right there. You know how you are doing. Take that assessment a step beyond that account balance looking back at you and think about how that makes you feel. How does the balance in your bank account make you feel?

When you think about how you feel, you begin to align your heart. Ask yourself: *What does my heart say? What did I hear when I listened to my heart?*

In the bank account example, you may feel differently if the number is a high versus a low balance. Rest assured, your heart will tell you exactly what you need to know—the good, the bad, and the truth.

I've been asked multiple times, "How do I know it is my heart talking versus my head—with my stress, worry, and fear—and why would I trust my heart?" Read that sentence back a few times and unpack it. It's all intertwined, but while your head is packed with subconscious programming, your heart is not.

In more than a few instances, my clients have produced decision charts. In one case, my client Tim took out a piece of paper and showed me the left and the right side of all the pros and cons—all thoughts and ideas, rights and wrongs, and yet he absolutely couldn't make up his mind. The pros even outweighed the cons. He was contemplating changing jobs. In discussing it with him, he said, "This is an impossible choice." I reviewed the list and said, "What does your heart say?" He said, "What do you mean?" I said it again: "What does your heart say?" He said, "My heart says, I'm miserable at this job and I want to move." I said, "Well, there is your answer."

You see, it really isn't that hard. You know what to do. It's just that the actions that go after following your heart are mostly back in your head and you begin to think things through. Stay in your heart and think with your heart, and the actions become easier. Tim knew he wanted to leave his job because he was miserable, so keeping that in mind and not losing sight of it, he began to shift course and make changes. He began looking for another job while having the "security" of this one. In just four weeks, he was hired at another company, which included a salary increase of 35 percent, better benefits, a shorter commute, and more fulfilling work. He did this while keeping the feeling as motivation and his heart-based thinking. When we overthink it, we may stay stuck, as all the reasons why we can't change—obstacles and how hard it is—may overtake our heart-based thinking if we don't keep listening to our heart while we implement change.

Here is another example. When I was recently working with my client Janet, she was saying she wanted to do a list of five things she had never done. Frustrated with herself, she hadn't done them already. Upon meeting me, Janet had said she wanted to lose seventy-five pounds, visit Hawaii, get a new job, save $25,000, and buy an income property, and her time frame was one year to do all those. It was an impressive list. When I asked her to cover her heart with her hands and give me the list again, she began crying. This time, she recited the list slowly, weeping, and she gave her reasons why she wanted to do what was on the list. She also left the last one out this time, as that was something her former husband, John, wanted to do. It wasn't really her dream. So we sat with the list and did the assessment at the end of this chapter, and Janet gave herself all scores of, on a 1–10 range with 10 being the best, a 3 and 4 with an 8 in the mix. The first assessment took Janet about an hour, with her writing notes and really thinking about it.

Janet had never been through this process, and as we went back through the numbers and areas and I asked her to think about the assessment from her heart and not her brain, her scores went from 3s to 6s and 7s with the 8 remaining an 8. Janet said in the first time doing this, she was actually thinking about how she felt others would score her, but this time through she would actually assess herself. So we went back and did the assessment again. This time Janet went all in with her own thinking that was more heart-centered. With heart-based, gratitude programs, Janet has now lost the seventy-five pounds and kept it off, Hawaii is on the radar, she has a new job, and $5,000 in the bank, and she's made a few new goals. Janet has put in the work and aligned with her highest, best self. It was transformative to see Janet begin to trust herself more and more, listen to her own self, and develop incredible confidence.

## SUCCESS TIP #3: Listen to Your Heart and Trust the Answers It Provides

Like Tim and Janet, you may be feeling like changing something or doing something a certain way for a reason. You may not have every answer, so listen and tune in. Sometimes these moments make for a great journaling session. The real reminder here, as you are having chats with yourself or others, is a phrase that I feel like I need to keep saying: "Trust your heart."

Over and over, I encounter those who have lost their heart hearing, often because they have been let down or feel fooled by following their heart, so they move into their heads and overthink. Sometimes we overthink everything so much we lose our passion and succumb to losing our way, thus also losing sight of the importance and beacon of light—*change*.

Keeping our heart-based thinking in mind, we are here to take a deeper look within with our first point of change and the process of assessing. Now, there are many kinds of assessments. Some are easy and routine, the ones you do without much thought. For example, we suddenly notice it's dark or darker than normal. We look up to notice a lightbulb is out. We change the lightbulb. All is right again. Same thing with the battery in a TV remote or filling up our car's gas tank. We have some simple changes that are generally a quick fix.

This got me thinking, and we had some fun in our house with this one. Feeling like Steve Harvey on *Family Feud* with the top five answers hidden on the board, I bravely asked, "What are things you routinely change and don't think much about it?" The number-one answer in our house was—drum roll, please—underwear. Oh, that's a mom's sigh of relief right there, and 150 people surveyed said the same answer. Then came this next line of thought, and let me tell you, it was a mom-of-four-boys' moment

I won't probably ever forget. In fact, this one is so bad it goes into Dad-won't-forget-either. Here goes: This is the moment we picked our oldest son up after his first year of college. We were helping him pack up his stuff and load the car, and I noticed the sheets were still on the bed. He said, "Oh, we should leave those; they haven't been changed." My husband and I glanced at each other, and I was the first to pipe up with this fine response: "Well, that feels like a waste of money. When is the last time you changed them?" If you think it was like a month ago and that would be a reasonable college response, keep reading. He said, "Oh, like September . . . of last year." Gross.

So what is that process going on in our heads when we know we need to change something and we don't? Sometimes it is the hassle factor or laziness, superstition if you ask a baseball player, or lack of a second set of sheets to put on while the other ones are in the laundry basket for the year. My lesson there was a decently firm reminder and monthly texts to our children: "Change Your Sheets, Love, Mom."

So from lightbulbs to hair color, socks, underwear, passwords, habits, mind-set—to maybe more difficult or complicated changes such as locations, jobs, relationships, homes, attitude, weight—the one thing that it all has in common is a moment of assessment, even a quick one, followed by action or inaction that fuels the success or lack thereof.

Often you can quickly assess a situation, make a choice, and that was that moment of change. Other require a more lengthy process, or while some are quick and routine, they may have ripple effects. Those are often my favorite ones. For example, you may open your refrigerator to take a mini assessment of what you need to buy at the store and go buy those things. That's change. However, more change may happen if at the store you see a new product you buy or you unexpectedly bump into someone you haven't see for a long time and you decide to get back in touch.

I think that's why staying highly tuned in to your surroundings and people is so important. It really is true that your life can change in a moment. May your heart guide you. I know mine has on multiple occasions. Your actions foster change and everything is always changing. You have the abilities to create lasting change within, to adjust due to circumstances, and to affect others in multiple ways. All of us are rippling change across the Universe, and some ripples are ones you never want to change. I get it. Please know that I have moments, and I'm sure you do as well, when I'll look around me and think, *I wish nothing would ever change.* Soon the moment changes. (Perhaps this is why I take so many pictures and videos.) I do know that years ago, by following the process in this book, I stopped allowing life to move me along like a current and largely being unaware. Today, I am much more aware of how my actions impact others and how I spend my moments. I clearly understand the value of time, from having nearly lost my life to allergic reactions and at other moments. I take my own assessment twice a year, using the tool provided at the end of this chapter.

## SUCCESS TIP #4: Ground Yourself in Gratitude

As you are assessing your life, root that assessment firmly in gratitude. For example, if you are using this book for a career change or life change, know that many climb the ambition ladder with no awareness. Be the one with awareness of others and do not become a trampler of other people's hearts, minds, and souls. Compassion becomes nonexistent when people run roughshod over others to get what they want without practicing conscious ambition. When you practice conscious ambition, you are allowed, of course, to want or need more and get what you want or need, but you go about it with respect for yourself and others around you.

So as you are assessing your life—with this book's exercises or anywhere else for that matter—hear my words: "May gratitude guide you." You can actually replace "gratitude" with any uplifting and powerful word. Say a few with me here:

May *love* guide me.

May *joy* guide me.

May *peace* guide me.

You get the drift. If you need to say it to others, please borrow it and say, "May love guide you," "May gratitude guide you," and so forth. These are wonderful phrases to give someone some direction with their heart in mind. Have conscious ambition practices rooted within you.

Be aware that we aren't all the same. We don't have the same experiences that have brought us to this moment, and we don't all have the same vibration or energy. We are all different and yet the same in so many ways that bring us together. Others are more aware and some less so, so be conscious of your heart and your time, as well as how you move around the universe with your heart guiding you to be aware of others. Surround yourself with love. As you encounter the souls who haven't yet learned this, be kind. When you see another who isn't behaving in a way that best appeals to you, apply love, kindness, and gratitude and maybe think of it like this: *They will be better for having encountered me.* While they may be the biggest jerk you've encountered to this moment, when you apply compassion, they are better for having encountered you. As for that moment, perhaps they haven't experienced what you've experienced, and your moment will guide them or change their course. Always remember that the person you encountered is someone else's child—or a wonderful love of their life, best caregiver, or so forth. So be kind; they just may not be for you. Conscious ambition creates the pause to guide you to make considerate and compassionate choices and behaviors.

I'd like to challenge everyone reading this to take a moment to champion others. Another person's win might be your best day! There is plenty of room for all of us to be happy and succeed. Herald and compliment others whenever possible. People need to hear it and be reminded.

As you do your best to encounter others with kindness, let's explore how you are encountering your own self. Let's move the focus back entirely on you.

## SUCCESS TIP #5: Pause and Assess the Situation Truthfully

When you are assessing anything, raw honesty is at play. If you aren't completely honest with yourself and others, well, what's the point, really? Raw honesty hides behind lies because we are afraid of what others might think or do, how they might react or respond or judge—and the list of why we mask our authentic selves plays on. We fear being shamed, blamed, or disliked, or worse, we feel like we don't align or fit in. It's okay. Align your heart to you and assess you and only you. Think about this:

- What's happening in my life?
- Am I feeling stressed or joy? Why?
- What am I saying to myself?
- What am I hearing?
- What am I feeling?

*So just what are you saying to yourself?* Are you kind to yourself? We must be our own champions.

Many times when people arrive with me for coaching, I'll hear "I really don't care what others think," or "I don't really care about myself." I have heard both of those statements more times than I care to remember! I'll think to myself, *Well, I think you are awesome!* In these moments, to help you connect back to yourself, sometimes it requires someone believing in you, maybe even more than you believe in yourself at that moment in time. Another's assessment of you might be so much better than you think. Going back to encountering others for a moment, know that your assessment of another might brighten that person's life.

So when you are lost, when you don't know what exactly to do, or when the answers aren't clear and things are foggy, please surround yourself with those who know the way. They are your champions and the people who believe in you. And then please, as they are giving you energy, be sure to fill up their emotional bank account with some kindness, appreciation, confidence, and compliments, so that they are not depleted. I'm sure a moment will come when they also need their reserves for their own moments or others'.

I've got to share this with you: In my younger years, I was probably not the most body-confident person. I'm getting better at this with age, but I still have my moments. When you meet me in person, know that on a big hair day I am just about five-foot-three. I am a former gymnast, and on me, every single pound shows. There just is nowhere for it to go. It's been a struggle at times.

However, I have learned to be body grateful as my body serves me well—for example, having given birth to four sons. I focus on gratitude and the positives, and my usual approach is to watch my health carefully. Well, in some moments of self-assessment in 2020, I realized I lost focus on my health to some extent during 2018 and 2019.

In June 2020, I stepped on the scale and nearly fell off it. I said to myself, *The cat is on here with me. No? Well, maybe all three cats are on here. No, maybe my husband put his foot on it and the joke is on me.* I stepped off and had a panic moment. It wasn't pandemic weight gain either. The moment of self-assessment was in fear of becoming more unhealthy. I even backed up and said that my overly snug, lumpy look in yoga pants prompted this, and as I stepped up again, I was hoping for a better number—but my heart knew. My head knew, too. Every part of me knew. I remember thinking to myself that I had let this go far too long and it was going to be impossible to reclaim myself. I was embarrassed.

It was a moment when I nearly folded up Best Ever You, feeling like I was definitely not my best ever anything. I was rather dramatic about it, feeling like I don't walk my talk and why would anyone listen to me ever or buy a book or on and on and on and on—terrible self-talk and several nasty self-moments. Truth and raw honesty here. I cried and felt like I had drifted so far from myself that my body wasn't going to cooperate to come back to what I feel is normal for me. But then a cool thing happened: my heart spoke up, and I heard it. I saw my original notebook outlining the points of change. I reconnected with my own process and knew in my heart instantly I was going to be sleeveless in summer and wear anything I wanted without head noise—but more so, I was going to once and for all figure out what was bugging me to yo-yo my weight ten or twenty for a few years. I told my business partner, Kris, that I was going to take ten to twelve days off and detox from caffeine, sugar, and salt, and to take over while I did this. It was a bit drastic, and let me tell you, the headaches were unreal the first few days, but I did it. I'll include more about this process as we go through the book, but I used my own coaching and practices that I used with others on myself, and it worked. As I write this, I am twenty-five pounds lighter and sleeveless in summer as wished, but more importantly, I feel so much better.

As you assess, if you aren't there yet in thinking you are the most wonderful, confident person, I am right here with you, and I've got a few people in this chapter who will believe in you until you are at that level of believing in yourself. Even if you are aware of being nice to yourself more often than not, we all have insecurities and unsure moments, especially with as huge a topic as change.

When you ask yourself, *Can I do that?* instead of answering, *I don't know, can I?* skip right to the words "I can." These will serve you well.

As we take these first steps in assessing our lives, we need to take a look within at how we are speaking to ourselves. Many a rut was started and fostered with horrendous self-chatter.

It's all in the way things are worded. A huge difference and shift in your energy take place when you say, "I'm grateful for the way I look." In my case, I said, "I'm incredibly grateful for this body that has given birth to four beautiful human beings and allows me to live and breathe." The whole energy and vibration of the way your entire being moves through all moments changes based on how you are speaking to yourself.

How others speak to you and their assessment of you can also be valuable tools. Others may see something in you that you just don't quite see yet. In the "Stories from the Heart" that appear in each chapter, you'll meet people just like you who have turned the ordinary into the extraordinary. In this first chapter, you'll meet Barbara Wainwright and Omar Kingston. These are two of the best and most incredible believers in others whom I know.

First let's meet Barbara, who has found her way to train and assist thousands of people, including myself, to become Certified Professional Coaches. Thanks to Barbara, I became a Wainwright Global Coach back in 2011 and in 2020 earned my Master Coach certification so that I now train others to become coaches. Barbara is masterful at helping others assess their lives, and being mentored by her is an honor.

# Stories from the Heart
## Barbara Wainwright, CPC—Transforming the World of Life Coaching

My name is Barbara Wainwright. I'm the CEO and founder of Wainwright Global, Institute of Professional Coaching. Since 2006, my company has trained and certified over 6,500 professional life coaches in the Wainwright Method of Coaching. Throughout this book, you are learning some of the tools and techniques we use to empower our clients and propel them to success.

Here's a quick share about my backstory and how I transitioned into the coaching industry.

I was a software engineer for many years. I owned and ran J. F. Positive Systems from 1985 to 2006. During my consulting years, I read a lot of books and attended classes and seminars on the topics of personal development, spirituality, psychology, metaphysics, and natural healing modalities. For the last ten years of that time, I had the intuitive push that I was supposed to do something other than develop software. I explored many different avenues, and nothing seemed quite right until I discovered the coaching world. I instantly knew that coaching was the path I had been seeking. It took me a few years of building my coaching business before I was able to fully transition from consulting to coaching full-time. Coaching was a completely different career—going from computer skills to people skills. However, I was committed 100 percent to staying on the path where my heart had led me.

As a software analyst/designer/developer, you need to be able to look at the big picture (the system) and also drill down into the details (bits and bytes). The ability to analyze and assess software and the needs of the end user seemed to apply to coaching individuals as I was assessing why people get stuck and what is needed to implement lasting change. In addition to my analytical skills, my research into psychology, spirituality, personal development, and metaphysics became a valuable asset when creating the Wainwright Method of Coaching.

When I looked at the big picture of coaching and accreditation, I discovered that it had been overcomplicated. Coaching isn't hard, yet some organizations had created courses that lasted for nine months or even two years. One accrediting organization requires 120 hours of training. When reviewing personal transformation and clients' needs, I was able to simplify the coaching process to help people get outside their comfort zone easily and naturally, so that their fight-or-flight stress response (self-sabotage) doesn't override their desire for positive change.

With coaching, you will learn how to encourage and motivate others to step into their greatness. It begins with an assessment. Are your mind and spirit in alignment? I believe that tapping into your life purpose and staying true to your heart are very important motivators. Meditation helps to clear the minutia from your mind so that you can discover and focus on what is most important. Are you taking care of your physical body? Are you feeding your soul? Do your habits enhance your life? Are you consistent with striving to improve? Are your actions congruent with your words? Are you trustworthy? Are you reliable? Do you finish what you start?

When asking yourself questions, pay attention to your language and the phrases that pop into your mind. You may be astonished at the disheartening messages stored in your subconscious mind. You may hear words like "never, always, everyone." Such generalizations most likely don't apply to you. Generalizations are misleading and are used to dissuade or manipulate someone (or yourself) from moving forward. Being specific in your communication with yourself and others will leave little room for your words to be misconstrued.

At the end of your day, take another assessment. Express gratitude for gifts received. From the perspective of your divine purpose, ask yourself, *Were my actions today in alignment with my goals?* Reviewing your day to discern if your actions were on point with your purpose is a personal growth technique that can pave the way for staying in alignment with your calling, which will result in both inner and outer success.

In our course, we teach coaches how to write a vision statement for their clients. The impact is a 100 percent wow! experience and results in great testimonials for the coach. A vision statement helps clients see themselves being successful. It helps to reprogram the subconscious mind to be in alignment with the creative conscious mind, which is a key factor in a client's success.

Over the years, I have witnessed many people receiving their vision statements. Their reactions are a combination of tears of joy; inspiration; feeling empowered, heard, and acknowledged; and an overall feeling that they will be successful. "Life-changing" is a comment I've heard frequently. I've had many clients call me and share that everything that was written in their vision statement came to pass. They are living their dream life and are so grateful that they had the experience of receiving their vision statement and the coaching that kept them accountable as they were moving toward their goals.

In this chapter, you are learning the importance of creating a vision statement and listening to it daily. My recommendation for creating your vision statement is this: First meditate to clear your mind. Let go of the past. Let go of what you've been told to do. Next, focus on your heart. Feel your heartbeat. Allow your heart to speak to you and to express its divine inspiration. Then write down what you are called to do. Know that the right doors will open for you when you are following this path. Imagine your best life. Imagine everything falling into place for you to easily accomplish your goals. Write your goals as if everything is already complete. Then record it and listen to it often. If a time comes when you are feeling off-center or stifled, listening to your vision statement will bring you right back to your center and will keep you focused on the result you wish to experience.

Namaste.

●  ●  ●

In the exercises that follow in this chapter, we begin looking at creating our vision statement, but first let's spend some time with Omar Kingston, one of the best fitness and leadership trainers in New England.

## Omar Kingston—Conquer the Everyday

I possess an energetic and complexly simple view to conquer the everyday. While orchestrating the physical tasks of being present for your family, work, and social circle, balancing the basic decisions to ensure you are being a good human must be ingrained in your behaviors. Our most undervalued commodity is time, and how we utilize and manage it should be heavily appreciated. As we seem to emphasize successes and social positions based on what levels in academia, sport, or business have been achieved, your foundation and then many subsequent factors will ultimately determine how the journey will unfold.

Growing up in the boroughs of NYC in the 1970s, my early exposures of life never fortified a concrete direction outside of football. While the love of sport magnified what many addressed as my identity, I meticulously and enthusiastically hunted for the peace of mind that accompanies the most traveled and well-rounded humans. While in sport, traumas and adversity may build strength, fortitude, and an ability to endure, true perseverance should come from the presence of a desire to learn, and subsequently a desire to develop within a calm place (environmentally or mentally).

During 2000–2001 my life began to make a shift. Now in hindsight, we all can recognize the magnitude and value of important times, but in the moment, they can seem trivial and even tedious. After losing my cousin and friend and separating from my wife, I became a single father of two young boys. Those traumas affected me, but the shift was truly felt during a trip to climb Mount Kilimanjaro.

I had built a business and reputation for my ability to use my experience in competing in high-level sport, and the patience to teach and help many advance to achieve many physical tasks. I was approached by a group to prepare them all for the climb. I agreed, with the only proviso being that I could join them. This, I knew, was an opportunity that I would be able to use to get a better grip on what I wanted my direction to be. On this trip, during which I successfully reached the summit, I was faced with my own insignificance in the world and simultaneously the immense value that I had to my children. At that emotional moment, I knew that my legacy would only be determined by the stories loved ones would tell regarding how I made them feel and the shared experiences. My legacy would definitely not be what I left for them.

Over the past two decades, I have helped thousands of athletes carve and structure their own journeys. The hunt for success and prosperity is layered with many unseen details. The ability to stay focused and driven is determined by how and what you have learned. The construct of the current status of "learning" is misinterpreted and loaded with misinformation to mask the actual work. Mimicking behavior without noticing and understanding the details of those witnessed behaviors or movements will never allow you to arrive with the same rewards. Those who help others master their own hunt possess many, many hidden talents and secrets that you should strive to learn. Let's discourage the easy road and quick return on investments because longevity of pursuit in any arena is irrefragable.

Be a good human.

● ● ●

Hang around Omar for about five minutes and you'll notice an immediate difference in your energy. By the way . . .

*Irrefragable*—such a great word. I'll save you a search if you needed one like I did: Definition—1: impossible to refute *[irrefragable* arguments]; 2: impossible to break or alter [*irrefragable* rules].

I feel so blessed to know Barbara and Omar personally, and I am so honored that they shared their stories so that we can learn from them. What did you learn? If you were to find someone near you who believed in you and your dreams, possibly more than you believe in yourself right now, who is that for you? If you don't have an answer at this exact moment, that's okay. Think about it while we take some action toward finding success in all areas of our life and aligning our heart, truths, and energy.

Both made me think about the moment in 2018 when my dad died, and for about a little over a year after I was fairly lost. I was grateful for my life and my health, but deep down something was really bothering me. After gaining twenty pounds, I took my own assessment, which you are going to do in Exercise 1. I felt like the grief and change were piling on as the last of our four boys went off to college. My husband, the cats, the dog, and I didn't really quite know what to do with the newfound time at first. The house was very quiet, and there was a lot less laundry.

To top it off, all around us, our friends were getting divorced. It was like the moment the kids left, people headed to the divorce attorney. It was a really strange feeling. We were great, but I am still me, and so I said out loud to my husband, "I don't want that to be us, and I can see the crazy changes all of a sudden. What should we do to avoid that?" Well, to keep this clean, I'll omit his first answer and just go with the second answer, which was travel. Fun! I was feeling like I needed to work on my professional career anyway, so armed with copies of PERCOLATE, we set to the airways. We even jet-setted up to Rochester to hang out with our son Quaid for his birthday!

Looking in from the outside, you'd never know anything was wrong, but on the inside, I knew I had a message, had grown, had another book to write, and had more to do and more lives to connect and couldn't see a clear path to do that. Then one of my author friends found Steve Harris and recommended me to Steve. Even as I first met Steve, I could see how hard it was going to be to pull myself up and understand I needed change. I was stuck. So know that the reason I know this process in this book works is that I and so many people I know use it. With all my might I decided to change my professional life, set some new goals, and take some new actions to alter my course. I also knew that I needed to take off those twenty pounds. So that was my assessment in that moment, and I gave myself a score of 4 in career and 4 in health. Ouch! A little hard on myself, but I'll share more on this adventure as we go through the chapters.

● ● ●

So are you ready for your own assessment?

On these next pages you'll find heart-based exercises titled "Points to Ponder." There are two exercises at the end of each chapter, and all the exercises compound and continue to the end of the book, playing off one another as we work through change. In these first exercises, you read a relaxation statement and then take a vision statement assessment. In the second exercise, I work with you to explore the language you use with yourself and give you some tools to help you be confident and kind in your approach with yourself.

Please know that if you don't want to write in the book, you can visit besteveryou.com/changeguidebook to print extra copies. As Barbara mentioned, as a Master Coach, in addition to training people to become coaches, I spend a lot of time creating vision statements for my clients and helping them process and make change or maneuver through circumstances. If you need assistance, please just ask. I'd be more than happy to guide you along the way to becoming a change master!

## POINTS TO PONDER

Think. Write. Talk. Action. *(Because practice makes us our best.)*

### EXERCISE 1: Let's Begin! Vision Statement Assessment

Let's take an honest assessment of what is going on in your life in multiple areas. This vision statement assessment is a first step in creating a vision statement for yourself, which illuminates a path of infinite possibilities.

In the areas below, please give yourself a score of 1 to 10. We do not allow zero as a score in this exercise. For each area in which you would like to experience change, please place notes or comments to briefly explain your score.

Here's an example:

#### SELF-LOVE, SELF-WORTH, VALUE

**Score:** 7

**Reason:** Sometimes I feel like I could be doing more to show myself love and acceptance for the choices I've made in my life that have led me to where I am today.

Before you begin, take a moment to get centered in your heart. This is an exercise of love. Love yourself enough to give an honest evaluation of where you are in your life. You may want to take a moment to read this relaxation statement once or twice. Focus your energy in your heart center.

### RELAXATION TUNE-IN

Take several deep breaths. As you take a deep breath in and out, imagine beautiful white light coming into your energy field from the top of your head down to your toes. Move your attention into your heart. Feel love and peace within your body begin to vibrate through your entire being. Taking another deep breath in and out, allow the energy of gratitude to emanate throughout your body: gratitude for everything in your life that has brought you to where you are today. Know that today you have the power to begin a change for the better. Taking another deep breath, staying present in your heart center, you are ready to begin.

## SELF-LOVE, SELF-WORTH, VALUE

Score: _____

Reason: _____

## OVERALL VISION OR PLAN FOR MY LIFE MOVING FORWARD

Score: _____

Reason: _____

## ACCOUNTABILITY FOR TAKING ACTION ON MY PLANS

Score: _____

Reason: _____

## OVERALL ATTITUDE OR OUTLOOK ON LIFE

Score: _____

Reason: _____

## SELF-AWARENESS

Score: _____

Reason: _____

## OVERALL WELL-BEING

Score: _____

Reason: _____

## CAREER

Score: _____

Reason: _____

## EMOTIONAL

Score: _____

Reason: _____

# SPIRITUAL

Score: _____

Reason: _____

# RELATIONSHIPS

Score: _____

Reason: _____

# FINANCES

Score: _____

Reason: _____

# GLOBAL CITIZEN

Score: _____

Reason: _____

# VOLUNTEERING

Score: _____

Reason: _____

# EXERCISE ROUTINE

Score: _____

Reason: _____

# NUTRITION

Score: _____

Reason: _____

# SENSE OF PEACE AND HARMONY

Score: _____

Reason: _____

# MIND-SET (STATE OF MIND: CUP HALF EMPTY OR HALF FULL)

Score: _____

Reason: _____

## PERSONAL AND PROFESSIONAL APPEARANCE

Score: _____

Reason: _____

## HOME AND LEISURE

Score: _____

Reason: _____

Great job! You did it!

Next, read this relaxation statement again before continuing on to Exercise 2.

## RELAXATION TUNE-IN

Take several deep breaths. As you take a deep breath in, imagine beautiful white light coming into your energy field from the top of your head down to your toes. Move your attention into your heart. Feel love and peace within your body begin to vibrate through your entire being. Taking another deep breath, allow the energy of gratitude to emanate throughout your body—gratitude for everything in your life that has brought you to where you are today. Know that today you have the power to begin a change for the better. Taking another deep breath, staying present in your heart center, you are ready to begin.

That's right! I now realize that I am very relaxed. In fact, the more I stop and take deep breaths, the more relaxed I feel. I am now aware that I am creating a harmonious environment every day in every way. Each and every time I stop and take deep breaths, I am already going beyond my normal experience, which causes me to recognize my infinite possibilities. That's right! I now recognize that I am grateful for my life, which feels increasingly great, and I now notice that my confidence has expanded exponentially.

## EXERCISE 2: The Language of Success!

When I coach people personally and professionally or when I certify people to become professional coaches, I spend a lot of time being specific with the language they are using in their everyday speech.

The language of self-love, self-worth, value, and confidence is powerful, and the language you use to speak to yourself or talk to others about your-self matters. One of the most powerful ways you can impact yourself in a positive way and affirm your vision for yourself is to change how you speak to yourself.

Do you speak to yourself as you would your best friend? Is your self-talk (the thoughts you think about yourself) congruent with who you see yourself to be? Are the words you hear in your mind and the words you speak of a high vibration and energy?

The right words foster success and train your brain to think positively and differently. The right words also move you toward your goals and help manifest your vision very quickly.

You can combine the power of words to form some amazing affirma-tions and power phrases to boost self-confidence, elevate your positive energy, and create lasting transformation and success. We use as many power words as we can in our vision statements.

Here is a power word bank. Consider circling the ones that resonate with you, sound good to you, or make you feel good. Circle the words that inspire you as you imagine embarking on this inner journey to change.

## MY POWER WORD BANK

| | | | |
|---|---|---|---|
| Abundant | Confident | Expanding | Impact |
| Accepting | Consistent | Experiencing | Increasingly |
| Accomplish | Courageous | Fabulous | Infinite |
| Achieve | Create | Fun | Inspired |
| Among | Creative | Generate | Joy |
| Awareness | Determined | Grace | Kind |
| Beautiful | Discover | Grateful | Love |
| Because | During | Gratitude | Loveable |
| Before | Easily | Happiness | Loved |
| Beyond | Energized | Harmonious | Magical |
| Causes | Energy | Heart | Magnificent |
| Claim | Enhanced | Imagine | Marvelous |
| Clarity | Exceeds | Immediate | Naturally |

| Now | Prosperity | Stop | I am aware |
|---|---|---|---|
| Peace | Purpose | That's right | I notice |
| Peaceful | Realizing | Unique | I now find |
| Possibilities | Resilient | I am already | I now realize |

Let's create some power phrases. Write in your journal or fill in the blanks with power words, either your own or those from the box.

I am _____ .        I create _____ .

I am _____ .        I create _____ .

I am _____ .        I create _____ .

I allow _____ .        I _____ .

I allow _____ .        I _____ .

I allow _____ .        I _____ .

You can even take this a step further and create powerful affirming reminders that support your vision. Say these a few times to yourself each day for thirty days. Try your hand at writing your own now.

Here are a few of my favorites:

I awaken each morning and now realize that I am very relaxed. That's right, I now feel more relaxed, safe, and at peace with the world than ever before. I am peaceful and relaxed.

Each and every time I stop and take a deep breath, I am already going above and beyond a normal experience, which causes me to recognize my infinite possibilities. That's right, I recognize that I am already living my dream life, and that feels increasingly great, and I now notice that my confidence has expanded. I allow peace. I allow joy.

Write your own affirming relaxation and power statement in your journal:

_____

_____

_____

Read your statement one to three times daily for thirty days or whenever you need an uplifting boost.

● ● ●

Congratulations! You completed Exercises 1 and 2. Let's continue to the next point of change.

# CHAPTER 2
# CHOOSE

*In this point of change, we practice choosing how we spend our moments and realize we are presented with a choice in how we want to be in each moment. In this point we act, create our new path and new reality, as well as establish real action steps toward this new you. You will commit to take these real steps to foster lasting change.*

**Everything we do cultivates and creates** our amazing life. What are you choosing? I was once at a baseball game where a father who was a coach on another team for ten-year-olds was talking on his phone the entire time in the dugout or when he was coaching first base. He did this all season. I'm not kidding. His phone would ring, and he'd take that phone call wherever he was on the field. Life is full of choices, and when his kid hit a home run that season, he had his back turned to the game and was over on the fence looking the other way. As the kid did the celebration jog around the bases and everyone was cheering, the father still didn't move from that position or his phone call. He missed the entire thing, even when things quieted down. He had absolutely no clue his son had hit a home run. To this day, I hope that was the most important phone call ever heard, as he heard nothing of what was happening around him. Of that I am certain.

In our second point of change, we are going to practice how we choose to spend our moments and realize we are presented with a choice in how we want to be in each moment. We realize in the present moment that everything we do cultivates and creates our future. When we make choices, we take action to create a new path, as well as establish real steps to be our best. So much of making confident, informed, moment-to-moment choices rests with mind-set and the power of conscious choices using your powerful, positive mind-set. How you view a choice may change if you decide to frame the situation with heart-based thinking.

Choice can be a mind-set of powerful intention and action so all that follows aligns to your heart, your truths, and your energy. There is power in choice, and that power rests with you. You are unstoppable if you choose to be. The possibilities are endless when you choose to see your life from a viewpoint of abundance. Sometimes you need to breathe, trust, let go, and follow your heart.

I often think of the choices I've made in my life. Some are great; others, not so fantastic. That's okay. I've learned to make better choices. I've also learned to hold my power and be confident in my choices and have learned decision techniques to support my vision for my life that I share with you. The choices I make need to align with my heart, my truths, and my energy to support my best version of me and the best possible life I can have. Personally, I like to find peace and choose peace. This doesn't mean I duck for the cover of solitude and try to stay oblivious to the happenings around me; it just means I don't often care to participate in the added drama. For me, it isn't peaceful. Peaceful to me might also not be what's peaceful for you.

One behavior I haven't found use for in my life is drinking. I just don't and really never had much of a taste for alcohol. I had a year of drinking my first year of college that honestly seemed enough for my entire lifetime.

The end of my drinking days was a moment I wish I could take back. I had partied all day long at an event and got on the bus to go home. I was not sober and was probably near alcohol poisoning levels. It was about an hour ride home, and as I stepped off the bus my dad caught me or I would have fallen and really hurt myself as I missed the bottom step. Then I threw up on him. My poor dad—and poor me. It was so not cool and a moment so to-the-core awful to me that I just don't drink anymore. I had a few other moments after that as I learned and became a person who is essentially a nondrinker or a mindful drinker for my entire adult life. I'll have a glass of wine on a holiday and that's really about it. It just doesn't serve me at all and never has. Nor do prescriptions (unless medically necessary) or other drugs. I am clean of everything but for a multivitamin, and that is my choice.

Ask yourself in this moment, *Who holds my power?* The answer is *you*. You hold your power. When we don't drift and lose sight of this, the power holds strong and can be developed stronger than ever.

## SUCCESS TIP #6: We Have a Choice in Each Moment

Mindfulness of your time and energy and how you spend it is key. One thing you can't do is *redo* your moments. As we make some new choices and try some new things, we need to remember that some things will turn out great, perhaps with a standing ovation, and others might not; that is okay. To help you have the most peace in your moment, in your choosing and decision-making, I have six go-to questions I use for myself and in my coaching practice. These will help you properly assess the situation and guide you to make the best choice possible when you are faced with change or want to make a change.

- Is this in line with the essence of who I am?
- Does this celebrate my unique gifts and talents?
- Do I take responsibility for my emotions, actions, and behavior?
- How does this impact others around me and the world as a whole?

- Does this moment or action contribute to my longevity and health?
- Is my mind at peace and my spirit content?

When you use these six questions, you align your heart and open the pathways to change.

## SUCCESS TIP #7: Stop Wishing for It and Start Working for It

Nobody can do your work for you, and a lot of effort can be involved. You are ready if you want to stop wishing for it and really start taking action and working for it. Your all-in attitude will help you succeed. This makes me think about attitude and perspective. When you have the best attitude you can have, combined with perspective, you have a better opportunity to frame your mind-set properly to make the best choices for your moments. In those choices, some will be heart based and some will be brain based, as different situations call for different ways of thinking and being. Alas, these are the choices we make.

As we make a choice to do the work, we learn we all need one another, and we trade off moments. We all learn from one another and have the opportunity to be lifelong learners with an open mind. Speaking of lifelong learners, in the last class I taught, I certified Deb Landry to be a professional coach. Deb is over sixty and a very respected leader in Maine. Deb doesn't have a know-it-all bone or gene in her body. She is made up of 100 percent lifelong learner. With that attitude of open-mindedness, Deb not only picked up a few new jokes in our class but she also found a new way of creating a vision statement for her clients and received her CPC certification. Yay, Deb!

"But, Elizabeth," you say, "I feel stuck!" I hear you. I feel you and I know. On the flip side of an open mind with a growth mind-set is a closed mind with a set of limiting beliefs. I know what it feels like to feel stuck. I can't talk about change without having a chat about feeling stuck. People are often stuck, paralyzed even. To get unstuck, you must begin to make choices and take action, but the trick is to be confident and stand behind the choices or actions you take. "Responsibility" is one of my favorite words because these moments involve taking responsibility for every aspect of our lives.

From owning and operating the Best Ever You Network over the years, I've helped many people get off their stuck hamster wheel and instead run toward a better and bolder life. When Kris Fuller joins me, you'll hear us both say, "Be brave, be bold, be you!" and we mean it. We wear T-shirts, have mugs, and have a journal, and we are champions of you becoming and remaining your Best Ever You! If this were a screenplay, we'd insert the championship music for you right here.

You are unique and incredible. With that in mind, I believe we need to have a chat about unforeseen circumstances. It takes incredible courage, a positive mind-set, and every Best Ever You tool in your toolbox to make changes or adjust positively to something negative that has happened. Because it can be so challenging to our entire being, change often feels like an incredible uphill climb with no clear direction. Where is the GPS for that?

The direction is within you. It is this process. It is looking at life in an infinite-possibilities mode. It is surrounding yourself with love and community and maybe even one day having a positive impact on others with your story. I feel your struggle. I hear stories daily of overcoming struggle and impossible circumstances. I look for them, actually, as they inspire me. From the stories about overcoming what is generally regarded as impossible to what you may feel is impossible, from overcoming the death of a loved one to finding your soul mate—to dealing with a medical disability on a moment-to-moment basis to getting up off the couch for twenty minutes a day to walk to the seventy-five-year-old finishing a degree to an author first published at age sixty-four, to 100-pound-weight-loss stories to people shifting from working in offices to entirely online and more, we often want to change something.

Change can be anything.

The trick is to take action, and the second step in taking action is to *choose*. You have a choice in each and every moment of contributing to how the moment plays out. In each and every moment you have an opportunity to be your best, and the responsibility for each moment rests within you and how you choose to bring it from within to external action.

● ● ●

When you choose to make a change or to frame an unforeseen circumstance in a positive light, you may need support. Maybe you need to acquire a new skill to facilitate this change. There is so much to think about when it comes to change.

To start, grab your coffee, tea, chocolate milk, or whatever suits you personally and shift into the land of unexpected grace. You are blessed beyond measure.

Hear me again: *You are blessed beyond measure.* Many of us forget that when we feel stuck.

Say it with me, slowly and with intention: "I am blessed beyond measure."

## SUCCESS TIP #8: A Vision Statement May Help You Change Your Life

A vision statement is a life-changing tool. As I mentioned, Dr. Barbara Wainwright, the founder of Wainwright Global, has personally mentored me since 2011. She taught me how to be a life coach, helped me with my first book, and certified me to become a Certified Master Coach so that I can train others to be professional coaches. I've worked with Barbara for years, and much of my work is rooted in her systems and the positive energy she brings to everything she does. Barbara has trained thousands of people to be the best coaches they can be and serve their clients with the highest of skills and integrity.

One tool we use, as I mentioned earlier, is a vision statement. Now, when I say "vision statement," what comes to mind? Many people think it's like a short mission statement, which is also great. Best Ever You vision statements are written individually for our clients. In this book, we help you create your own version with some of the same processes we use when coaching others. I am vision-statement crazed. I have used them for years to achieve my own goals and used them for years with my clients also as a highly successful tool.

I think *everyone* should have personal and professional vision statements! I also think they should be revised at least every six months. Our process in coaching people one-on-one differs slightly from what we present in this book, since we are not writing the vision statement for you. With our clients, we write the vision statement, read it multiple times, and even record it so that our clients can listen to it. The statement includes power words, phrases, and sentences that help our clients remove limiting beliefs and subconscious lines of thinking that are no longer serving them properly.

A well-written vision statement celebrates you and guides you in your daily choices. It provides encouragement and the direction necessary to chart the course for your best life. Your personal vision statement illuminates a path that is full of infinite possibilities! It removes limiting beliefs, roadblocks, and other obstacles we put in our paths that potentially limit our success. The Best Ever You process helps you take control of your destiny. By crafting realistic goals and taking an honest look at where you are currently and where you want to go, this powerful process ignites your internal passion.

Here are two examples of vision statements that some of our coaches wrote for one another as they were becoming certified. With their permission I've included them here for you to read. Please keep in mind as you read that these statements are designed for their ears, so during the vision statement assessment and interview process, our coaches are trained to listen for phrases clients use and we repeat their wording back to them using neuro-linguistic programming (NLP) practices. We tell our clients to read a relaxation statement to put their mind in the proper place to hear their vision statement and then listen to a recording of their vision statement at least once daily, often before sleeping. We've even had clients leave the recording on while they are sleeping with efforts to reprogram their subconscious mind. I love it!

This is Deb's vision statement prepared by Cheryl.

> Deb, it is a wonderful day and life is good. Your power words are Determined, Inspired, Honest, Respectful, Caring, and Loving.
>
> Deb, you feel relaxed, calm, centered. Because you are determined and inspired to be the healthiest version of you, you now are realizing your dreams with vitality, enthusiasm, and exuberance. As you have a huge support system—a husband who anticipates your needs, children who love and respect you, and because you know that people can do amazing things when they are supported—you now are able to definitely meet your goals.
>
> Because your desire is to enjoy movement, you committed to a full year with a health coach, walked your dog, River, played golf, used your TRX, stretched, meditated, and made your health a priority. You've lost thirty-five pounds and naturally feel great. Your newfound love of exercise has opened up the possibilities of being able to be more healthy, do more, and in turn you will live longer to watch your grandchildren grow. Whatever you put your mind to, you get what you want. You now realize that you have the ability to reach any goal you set for yourself.
>
> Because you listened to your health coach and utilized your resources to attain your goal, you naturally feel more confident in what you wear and allow yourself to buy clothes and strut around so that others will wish they were you. The possibilities are endless.
>
> Because you are clairvoyant with a special talent for analyzing dreams, you have become more intuitive. You journal your thoughts and reflect. You now go with your gut and are more in touch with your feelings. This makes you feel more confident and open-minded, which feels good.
>
> Because of your intrinsic desire to be the best in your

profession, you built a business that exceeded expectations and continues to grow with your new ideas and directions, must-have products, and expertly building and maintaining relationships. Your ability to run the operational side of a business provides the structure and rules set in place for others to feel safe, harmonious, and welcomed. Your caring, loving, honest, and respectful nature play an infinite part in making others want to belong to any team you are leading. You are worthy of all recognition from others.

Because you have planned for your future, you can do work you enjoy and stay semiretired. By having money in the bank and investments, you now realize you easily have the ability to live the life you want, which includes travel and dining out with friends and family who are positive and have the same high standards as you. Your relationships are strong as you have boundaries, communicate, and surround yourself with those you love. You feel satisfied.

Summary:

Deb, your desire to enjoy movement has opened up a new world of possibilities. You know you will live longer, feel better emotionally and physically, and no longer be held to society's standards. You can accomplish anything, as you have done so in every aspect of your life. Deb, you are an inspiration and an amazing human.

● ● ●

During our time together in this book, we help you craft a personal or professional vision statement akin to this one, but first let's give one more example. This is Cheryl's vision statement prepared by Deb.

Cheryl, you are at peace when in nature. Your Power Words are Determined, Confident, Inspiring, Achievement, and Strong.

Cheryl, you are a resilient, strong, and determined woman living an extraordinary life. You feel relaxed, calm, and centered when exercising, walking, and on Sundays when you spend the day with your family. Sundays at home is your Zen place. Because you balance work and home life, you now meet your needs and have a guilt-free life.

You now are realizing your dreams with enthusiasm and excitement to become the executive director of your new international pageant system. You now will have enough money to help Abbey through college and retire at an earlier age of sixty-three.

Cheryl, you are now living life with a clear conscience and have clear professional and personal boundaries. That's right! You are now able to live a calm, relaxed life, and naturally you sleep peacefully at night.

As you love to help others, you now notice that you feel incredible and so grateful as you assist young women in finding their passion.

Because you declined extra volunteer jobs and because you have set boundaries on your limitations professionally by taking a leadership role in solving personnel issues for your job, your boss realizes your potential and respects your boundaries. With your extra time, you now have time to relax at your lake house and spend more time in your Zen place, relaxing and enjoying your family.

Cheryl, the support of friends and family is abundant, and you have time for them and—more importantly—time for yourself to provide self-care.

You love having your finances in order, and now that you have hired a financial advisor, you feel secure, wealthy, and relaxed.

Cheryl, your newfound clarity has rid all thoughts of doubt because you know you have a heightened awareness of truth. You now are able to focus on yourself in a healthy, loving way.

You are now free to efficiently work in your gardens, sit by the lake or fire, and enjoy the company of your loved ones or read a novel.

Because you now feel in control emotionally and

professionally, you remind yourself every day that you are an amazing, caring, determined woman who loves life.

You now realize that you can achieve all your dreams.

Cheryl, because you have a close relationship with your family, you feel loved with a deep sense of compassion, understanding, and support.

You are energetic and enthusiastic. You are so excited because you have had inspiring discoveries and vacations, taking Abbey to every state in the United States. You feel fantastic, and you are aware of how great it is to have fun.

Because you are now disciplined and have made it a priority to set goals and achieve them, you now have money for fun adventures, and because you are focused and resilient, you are now debt-free.

Your conscience is clear, and you notice your self-esteem and confidence increasing every day.

You now stop and take a deep breath and realize you feel healthy and calm. You meditate every day, which reminds you to take time for yourself, and you take time to relax in other ways. You are a compassionate and kind person.

You are setting an excellent example of what a strong woman is, and this reflects in Abbey. You love to cook and teach. You feel satisfied and loved.

Summary:

Cheryl, you have easily experienced and completed your incredible financial, personal, and professional goals. You have fulfilled your dreams, allowing you to create new possibilities for your future, retirement, and education for your daughter.

● ● ●

Now also for Cheryl, I've included her personal assessment. Cheryl ranked herself in six areas with these scores, and we listened for her power words and listed them as well.

## ASSESSMENT SCORES

Professional: 8                          Emotional: 8

Financial: 8                             Relationship: 8

Spiritual: 3                             Health and Wellness: 8

## POWER WORDS

Determined                               Achievement

Inspired                                 Strong

Confident

You'll notice Cheryl gave herself a 3 in the spiritual category. When asked what area of her life she wanted to focus on, since all were higher rankings, she asked to specifically focus on spiritual practices that would contribute positively to her overall well-being.

These are examples of work we have done with clients we've recently certified to become life coaches. Doing a vision statement doesn't mean you need to become certified. In this case, we were teaching Deb and Cheryl how to write and deliver vision statements for their clients and taking them through the process themselves so they could take away a bit extra from the course.

From the vision statement process, we move on to setting goals and taking action. I believe and have witnessed that people tend to accomplish goals, dreams, plans, and visions when they have them written down and also vocalized. It is very important to share this information with others so that people can show up for you and assist you. Imagine the teams assembled to bring together someone's vision for a full-length movie. It starts as an idea and then moves from there until you see all the details on the screen.

Such beautiful vision statements from both of these women just make me smile. Did I mention that Deb and Cheryl are mother and daughter? What an amazing honor it was to certify both, and during the many hours we spent with them, we were cherishing the moments they spent together learning. It was truly something to be part of, and Kris and I are grateful for the time with both Deb and Cheryl.

I really love these next two stories about choice. Please meet our youngest son, Quaid Guarino, and Brian J. Esposito. Both share stories of how their lives changed through pivoting and making powerful choices.

## Stories from the Heart
### Quaid Guarino—What Was Meant to Be

Choice and decision, especially at an early age, play a major role in how we define ourselves. My first major life choice came in June 2018. I had just finished my sophomore year of high school when I felt like I needed something different in my life. I was not satisfied, nor did I feel like I was being challenged in most aspects of my life. After years of feeling that way, I decided to graduate high school one year early. I knew it would be a challenge, but I was determined to accomplish my goal. I loaded up my schedule and prepared for the college admission process. It did not go as I had anticipated; I was rejected at 88 percent of the schools I applied to despite having a top 97 percent SAT score and a 97.3 GPA. At first I had my sights set on the New England Small College Athletic Conference (NESCAC) schools, but those dreams were crushed quickly. By late December I was getting worried and stressed out, but at 10:42 PM on January 14, the last day before applications closed, I got an e-mail from Rochester Institute of Technology offering me a fee waiver to apply. I quickly jumped on the opportunity because I thought to myself, *Why not, what is the worst that could happen? Another no?*

By mid-April I had received all my college decisions. I was rejected at twenty-three of twenty-six schools. It was between New Haven, University of Maine, and Rochester Institute of Technology. I chose RIT because it was unknown to me; it offered me a chance to elevate myself intellectually and to grow in a challenging academic environment. I arrived on campus in fall 2019 and began to thrive. I had stumbled upon an amazing biology program and found my passion. Classes were going great, and I had branched out. I found a passion in rock climbing, bouldering, and playing spike ball, and even made dean's list my first semester. But when I went back home for winter break, I felt that I wanted more and I chose to get the most out of what college had to offer. When I came back for the spring 2020 term, I loaded up my credit hours and began pledging the Phi Kappa Psi fraternity. I felt like I was finally starting to make something of myself. I was ecstatic and over the moon about where I was in life. Spring break at RIT was rapidly approaching, and for break I went to North Carolina with my parents to watch my brother play college baseball. Life was going great, and then the COVID-19 pandemic struck the world. I did not know how much the pandemic would change my life.

I spent the rest of the spring semester struggling with my classes because neither my professors nor I knew how to make the right decisions in how to adapt to the unprecedented situation. I finished with an all right GPA that semester, but what was most important was the fact that I had accomplished what I was determined to do. I was challenging myself and growing as a person faster than I could have ever imagined.

Surrounded by the brotherhood and opportunities of my fraternity, I made the choice to start taking on leadership positions, to minor in history, and to make a difference in my communities, regardless of how big or small they are. I was elected as a committee head and executive board officer in the fraternity during the fall 2020 semester. I was helping to lead a team of driven and successful men while being able to learn from them and the other leaders. The previous executive board and the one I was a part of worked diligently and ultimately won the Grand Chapter award from our national organization, meaning that New York Theta was the best chapter of Phi Kappa Psi in the nation for 2019 and 2020. I felt validated in the choices I had made when the announcement for the award came. I knew I was making the right choices to make myself better. The path I had laid out for myself was being realized.

One of the things I learned along the way was that the only thing that can stop you is yourself. Motivation and perseverance, through the obstacles you encounter while going through the labyrinth that life can be, are the keys to success and building yourself up to where you want to be. There is a choice at every intersection in the maze. Do you keep working at your goals? Do you stay complacent? Do you give up? Do you build up your foundation? What do you do when there is no right way to navigate the maze, when the right path feels like it is hidden? You make the choice to push on toward your goals. It might be a new goal, the same one from when you were a kid, a monumental achievement, or even something as simple as making your bed. Whatever it is, you have to make the choice to be better every day, no matter how big or small the improvement is. Small amounts of progress are still progress and eventually they add up. Ultimately, the choice is yours to guide yourself through the maze and find a path through because each path leads you to achieving your goals.

## Brian J. Esposito—A Million-Dollar Choice

Oh, what a journey it has been, and there is not a day that goes by that I do not regret one of the most life-changing decisions I ever made, which was to turn my back on my one true love and passion, what I lived, breathed, and ate: baseball. It was October 5, 1999, when I made a conscious decision at the age of eighteen to give up the sport and focus on building my professional career. This decision was after giving a large portion of my life to this beautiful sport, training every day for almost ten years as well coaching kids' baseball camps with Major League Baseball players for five years. It was the hardest of times, and it was the best of times. My dedication, hard work, and drive had led me to receive a full scholastic and baseball scholarship to St. Joseph's University, and my path was in place, but something was missing. During that time, I had to deal with an unusual amount of stress, setbacks, and "games" at my high school—a school where I was an outsider when I transferred in yet worked hard to earn the friendship and trust of my entire class, for which I humbly became senior class president. I bring this up not to brag but to touch on my abilities to connect with people across all kinds of interests and cultures—a strength that I had no idea how powerful it was until things really started to kick in later in my life. There were very unfortunate incidents with my high school coach and certain players that led some to even end their lives, and my skills were never enough to get the support and acknowledgment a young adult needs to give oneself not only confidence but certain levels of pride. I was surrounded by chaos, noise, disappointment, and sadness. Even after a 1998 spring tournament trip to Cooperstown, where I had one of the most exciting moments of my life on that gorgeous Doubleday Field, where I hit a double, triple, and home run, and even turned what looked like an impossible double play at second base. I actually felt possessed, in a good way, with some of the great baseball legends of the past during that game.

Moments like that are supposed to be fueled and become a new base from which you can build excellence. However, that was not the case—but I'm grateful for learning at an early age to not expect things out of life, that life is hard; to appreciate the now; and to enjoy as many wonderful parts of this journey as we can. That day also became the mantra of what I was set to do and I focused on a few very key powerful words: "Time is our most precious commodity."

When I hung up my cleats for the last time, I decided I was going to bring with me into this next chapter of my life all the wonderful things that this sport taught me, which were leadership, teamwork, hard work, and drive, and to not only appreciate the wins, but also analyze and study the losses. I transferred to Monmouth University, close to home, graduated in three and a half years with a business marketing degree and minor in psychology as well as ran a famous local coffee shop, the Inkwell, where legends like Bruce Springsteen, Kevin Smith, Danny DeVito, and Bon Jovi would frequent. I was going to class six days a week—eight in the morning until five at night—then running the late-night coffeehouse and restaurant until 4 AM along with my brother, and rinsing and repeating every day. The place had so much energy, talent, and success; to this day there is still nothing like it, and the lines we would have around the block were simply amazing. I quickly learned at that spot what great marketing, great service, a great product, and a legendary brand and name can do, but more importantly what a team can do! Again, the second I decided to give up the physical sport, I made it very clear to myself that I was going to bring what I loved about baseball into my personal life and professional career. Every business I started, opened, and built into my holding company had to have some core principles in order for me to believe it had a chance to succeed. It had to have the right brand and story (the team name and structure); the right product(s) or service(s) the market demanded (a team that could execute); a good understanding of the landscape and competition in the market (opposing teams and divisions); the right people leading it and strategically put in the right positions (there are nine players on that field, all skilled at their position; you should not have someone who would be best at third base playing catcher); not only the right manager, but also the right general manager, trainers, as well as the right owner(s); and more importantly, it had to find a way to connect to the customer (the fan).

My life has been hard for me. I have always accepted that, and I know more hardship will follow, but I've learned that I do not need acceptance from anyone, I don't need anyone to be proud of me, except myself, and I am here on this planet to leave a positive mark. There are now presently seventy-four holdings in my holding company, accompanied by over 150 joint ventures from around the world and operating in over twenty-five different industries. I finally love what I do. I finally feel a sense of worth about being able to take what I have built—which is my companies, partnerships, resources, relationships, experience, and strategic way of thinking—and be able to work with start-ups, and even Fortune 500 companies, where we create real value. I love being able to show companies how to succeed, become self-sufficient, and establish real revenues with positive earnings and cash flow. That is how you grow a company, and that is how you succeed. There are no shortcuts in life—and the harder the journey, the more rewarding the outcome. But with all that, very rarely does someone find something they truly love, and when you find that, do not give up on it. I found a unique way to bring in aspects of a game that I was born to play, and I'm manipulating some aspects of that game in my life, but it will never be the same. I know I would have been happy making $6,000 a year playing single-A baseball somewhere, but rather than constantly playing Bruce Springsteen's "Glory Days," I decided to find another way to make something of myself, and reminisce occasionally of a time I was grateful to have, with a sport I'll never forget.

● ● ●

Again! More incredible stories of how moments of choice that align with your heart, truths, and energy help you find success. What did you learn from these two stories? What are some important choices you've made in your life? Have you ever made choices that weren't popular with those around you? How do you navigate choices that involve really big goals or dreams?

Their stories make me think about choices and the vision statements I've used in my life. I have a new vision statement about every four to six months, depending on the goal or what is going on in my life. I've had a few years where I used the same vision statement, but since 2011, I've seldom been without an updated one. Late 2017 and all 2018 are what I call "My period without a vision statement." I was a bit lost and here is why.

I'll start with the choice I made in late 2017 and one that was made for us as a family. Late 2017 was an up-and-down period. The up was the kids. Life was good. We were enjoying wonderful success; our sons were all doing well; we were doing well—until life had other plans. I decided I needed to go home to spend a lot of December with my parents in Minnesota. Deep down, in my heart of hearts, I knew that it was going to be my last Christmas with my dad. He knew, too. He was a stroke survivor since 2004 and I wrote extensively about him in my first book *PERCOLATE*, as his will to survive and keep his faith was remarkable. The nurses affectionately called him the ICU Warrior.

For my visit, he mustered up all the energy he had, and I stayed for around ten days or so. I'll never forget him saying, "It must be quite something to see your dear old dad like this." I said, "You're alive. That's what I care about." He said, "Well this is my last Christmas. I am dying." It was heartbreaking, but it was the truth, and it was his way of saying, "Talk to me while you can." I have his voicemails and I of course saw him in the hospital in 2018, but that was the last hug I had from my dad. So, please, when you think about the choices you make and your vision for this or that, be very mindful of your time and how you place your energy, as your moments are precious. You don't get to redo them. Follow your heart. My dad, James F. Hamilton, was in the intensive care unit at a hospital in Edina, Minnesota, on and off, for most of 2018. At one point, my sister Alex gave birth to their baby girl Andie on one floor of the hospital while my dad came in through the emergency room. They were in the hospital at the same time on different floors and departments. There's no vision statement I have ever used that plans for that. No vision statement says, "Let's choose a path so he stops suffering or let's plan a funeral." I did need a new vision statement to shake the memory of picking out the urn. I'm still stunned at the urn selection and what I had the potential to do with our dad's ashes. It's not my thing to make a lamp or necklace or whatever from them, and I found it mortifying and is not something I even knew existed. I want that day out of my brain still. I can't unsee or unhear it. My husband and I also helped pay for the urn and some funeral expenses, and I have difficulty unseeing me pull a credit card out of my wallet and paying that expense. It's just very odd.

So, thank you for listening and hearing me here, as it's a moment where I could have been stuck—stuck in grief. By mid-2019 I was ready for a new assessment, a new vision statement, and some new goals. It was time to write a new book—and that's what I did.

When you lose your way, which happens, it is important to forgive yourself and your imperfections. Not every moment is the best, but you can be your best even in those moments.

Let's wipe our tears, and as my wonderful friend Sally Huss says, "Carry on." Carry on I must do, as my dad, in that moment, said for me to "put one paw in the front of the other and continue on." Without him. Instead, I am moving forward with *you*. If you are here and you've lost a parent, a friend, a family member, a pet—whatever or whomever—I'm here with you. We've all lost a lot in 2020–2021, for example, and we are choosing to move forward. We are adjusting. Adjusting is a choice.

The Ten Points of Change allow for those maneuvers through life, and we expect them. The fact that you will most likely make adjustments, I hope, doesn't stop you from making a choice you want to make. It's likely to be better than indecision or avoidance or other low-vibrational energy such as procrastination. Those all rest with not knowing the exact outcome ahead of time. What if you have a positive outcome? What if you place your energy and thoughts in a best-case scenario, where hard work pays off and things work out? Make the best possible choice you can for the best possible moment and make the best of your moments, for they are precious.

Let's move on to Exercises 3 and 4. In Exercise 3, you are going to choose an area of your life to focus on to change. In Exercise 4, we are going to write a vision statement by completing some information. Remember, in personal coaching, this is something we usually write for our clients and read to them. These exercises have you doing this yourself. If you need assistance, please reach out and I'll be happy to help you.

## POINTS TO PONDER

**Think. Write. Talk. Action.** *(Because practice makes us our best.)*

### EXERCISE 3: Choose One Area

In this exercise you're going to select the most compelling area in which you would most like to change for the better.

In your mini life assessment in Exercise 1, where you scored yourself from 1 to 10 in several areas, please identify the areas where you scored the lowest. Write them in your journal or below.

1. Area: _____ Score:_____

2. Area: _____ Score:_____

3. Area: _____ Score:_____

4. Area: _____ Score:_____

5. Area: _____ Score:_____

Of these five areas, which one would you most like to change? To help you get clarity, here's a relaxation moment for you. Do this process for each area you have listed.

### RELAXATION TUNE-IN

You may want to take several deep breaths. As you take a deep breath in, imagine beautiful golden light coming into your energy field from the top of your head down to your toes. Move your attention into your heart. Feel love and peace within your body begin to vibrate through your entire being. Take another deep breath and bring in one of the areas you listed above. Take a deep breath and ask your heart, *Is this the most important area to work on?*

Repeat this process for each area in your list.

Taking another deep breath, staying present in your heart center, you are ready to choose. Circle the area you choose to change now.

Write it here: _____

# EXERCISE 4: Your Choice, Your Vision

Next, since we love action and not just words, we are going to craft our personal vision statement. When finished, read this statement to yourself daily at least once per day for thirty days.

Area: _____ (from Exercise 3)

It is important to me to focus on my _____(area)
because _____
_____.

One goal I have is _____
_____
_____.

Another goal I have is _____
_____
_____
_____.

When I imagine I have already reached my goal, I feel _____,
and my success looks like _____.

To reach my goal I need to keep thinking _____, _____,
and _____.

One action I am willing to take is _____
_____
_____.

Another action I am willing to take is _____
_____
_____
_____.

One roadblock to my success is _____
_____
_____
_____.

I am going to take this specific action to work around this roadblock:
_____
_____
_____.

That's right, I am _____, and I am _____.

That's right, I allow _____, and I also allow _____.

That's right, I create _____, and I create _____.

I am loved. I am peaceful. I am joy.

I am _____ [your name].

# CHAPTER 3
# DISCOVER

*In point 3, we practice discovery. Like a scientist taking new data or a consumer tasting a new blend of coffee, this is where we learn about ourselves to establish values, goals, and beliefs and start to put that in line with our behavior. This is also where we learn a new skill, lesson, or talent.*

**Remember that sometimes you must ramble,** wander, explore, talk, connect, share, trust, and more to get to your point, mission, or whatever it is you seek. Trust yourself. Keep going. Never give up. It feels to me that we always have something new to discover about ourselves. Whether it is something learned in a moment or something done that produces other results and more discovery, I believe we are moment-to-moment, lifelong learners.

I teach people to anchor in their power and root in gratitude. When you do this, you really create a foundation, and you know some things for certain about yourself. I call them constants. For example, for me, not liking lima beans is a constant. Sorry, lima bean fans, but yuck. Another, perhaps more useful example for me that is a constant is that I help people get results, often when overcoming a change they didn't ask for. I know this is a strength of mine. I know I have helped multiple people make changes in their lives and find success.

Also, natural gifts and talents play a role in what we do with our lives and often this is discovered at a very young age. As parents of four sons, my husband and I have tuned in to pay attention to what our children loved to do from an early age. As a toddler, Quinn loved the sky, weather, and stars. He is getting his master's degree in Geoscience and Applied Meteorology. Our oldest son, Connor, has always enjoyed discovering the uniqueness of others. He has a leadership role at his job and continues to develop, grow, and mentor others. Our son Quaid has shown an aptitude for science since kindergarten and is now studying biology in college with hopes of becoming a doctor.

Our son Cam began tossing a ball around at the age of eighteen months. He is now a lefty pitcher playing at the college level. In high school, which now seems like forever ago, he was a Gatorade Player of the Year in Maine 2017.

Whether you get the blue ribbon or the accolade or whatever it is, remember they are testaments to your personal growth and discovery: your story, your life, and your moments. It is important to connect and reconnect with your natural gifts and talents on an ongoing basis. In my experiences in coaching people, I often help people remember what they love to do or naturally excel at but have lost sight of it.

You can anchor and grow with your gifts and talents and pass your knowledge forward to others. For example, this past summer, Cam led a baseball camp all week long, each day, with fifty-three six- to twelve-year-olds. This experience helped him grow with his own personal coaching experience and helped the kids grow in their baseball journey. Cam continues to discover what he can do when given the opportunity to do so.

In this chapter, we discover.

## SUCCESS TIP #9: When We Practice Discovery, We Allow

Discovery is a point where we learn about ourselves to establish values, goals, and beliefs and start to put those in line with our behavior.

We all have these constants. We may lose sight of our constants or we may lose our passion for them, but they are our constants. You know them to be true for you. What are some things that are absolutes for you?

Another mind-set tool I use is to help people anchor in a power moment, as I'll do here with you. You hold your power. If you are seeking change and want to align with your highest purpose, the power is in your hands.

## SUCCESS TIP #10: Anchor in Your Power

Please pause with me and place your hands over your heart. As you do this, please think about a moment or time in your life when everything was really going well. You were maybe feeling like you were on top of the world, everything was going your way, and you were very happy. Have you got that moment in your mind? Now, as we go through this chapter, please hold that memory or moment with you. I'll refer to it as the discovery point. I'd like to ask you to now recall that moment or memory and say, "I am grateful for the moment or memory when _____."

At this point, you as a person are grounded in gratitude. You have accomplished or achieved or been, and so you know you have the power, even when you feel lost or stuck—sad or worried or anything less than happy or joyful—and need internal or external strength, even if for just a moment. This is a discovery point.

For me it's life. I really make an effort to root in gratitude each morning. When I wake, I am grateful. I know what it feels like to nearly lose my life, and that perspective makes that moment very special. Being a person who has had multiple life-threatening allergic reactions created a perspective for me to cherish deeply things many take for granted. I root in gratitude, and so can you with the small exercise we just did. I am grateful for the moment when I survived. That is the real point at which I decided to ground in gratitude.

As you root in gratitude, let's chat about what you want more of. Now more than ever we need to discover what truly matters the most to us. Since opening Best Ever You, I've always had a practice of what I call "Tossing Spaghetti Around."

## SUCCESS TIP #11: Toss Spaghetti Around

It's a process by which I toss a lot of things into the Universe to see what sticks. Sometimes when you do this, however, nothing feels like it is sticking. You may have the best idea in the world, toss it up al dente style, and it just doesn't stick or, become popular, ever heard of, or seen. You endlessly feel like you aren't successful. In business you can throw out that idea and toss that spaghetti around, and it can become your process and way of doing business.

About fifteen years ago, I remember having a crazy idea that my husband should work from home more. We both felt like he was going to miss a lot if he didn't do something different. Since that moment, he has always had a job that was based from home. He has not missed a game, play, concert, or any moments for the kids or me. Not one. He takes great pride in this, and I share that pride as it hasn't always been easy. I knew looking around at all the hustle and bustle and commutes, this would ultimately serve him better, and so did he. Fast-forward to him being very frustrated with his job, I remember looking at him and saying that we needed to go back to owning our own company again. This time, I felt, it needed to be different, so I went thinking, noodling, doodling, and Googling—my four favorite things to do when I need to come up with ideas.

I remember tossing spaghetti around when my husband and I wrote the business plan for Compliance4. In the moment when we looked at each other and said, "That's it!" I added, "Four can be the number of children we have." He added, "It could also mean whatever compliance you need and for everyone." A-ha! He added his mom's famous sauce and some meatballs to my crazy spaghetti idea. Collaboration! And in that moment, Compliance4 began. That night we created the logo and registered the domain. The next day we created language for the website and ordered business cards and magnets. Everything was running in two days, and our first client came within two weeks. We began to flourish within the first year and are so grateful we made the leap into owning our own business.

Can you visualize your idea or goal? What do you see, hear, and feel? Now sometimes when I ask those questions, people don't understand. *What do I hear?* It could mean that you no longer hear the honking of horns in endless two-hour traffic, sitting on a bus to and from Boston each day, because you own your own business from home. It could mean you hear the jet roar as you take off on vacation to California. You feel free. You feel relaxed. You feel success.

I posted a picture on LinkedIn that was my commute one day. It was from my patio door to my pool. Not all days are the same, of course, but on that particular day, I rooted in that moment and in gratitude. I took the day off to chillax, and that was my way of feeling success—much-needed day off.

As you discover, toss your spaghetti, and learn more, this next tool may also help you. I created this in 2008 when I started the Best Ever You Network, and we still use it today. It's called the Best Ever You Principles. Originally there were five, and today they are called the Six Best Ever You Principles. In 2020, Kris Fuller and I put words to paper and created a better framework around them, and then, with the help of author Jennie Lee, we added a sixth principle: spirit.

## SUCCESS TIP #12: Learn the Six Best Ever You Principles

### PRINCIPLE 1: THE CORE OF YOU—YOUR VALUES ZONE

**Focus point:** This is the essence of who you are, including but not limited to your values, goals, beliefs, and behavior.

**Guiding Action:** Live life with strong, unwavering values and character.

**Ask yourself:** Is this in line with the essence of who I really am? Is it my truth?

## PRINCIPLE 2: THE ART OF YOU—YOUR INSPIRATION ZONE

**Focus point:** This is your unique and authentic self and enables your contributions to the world.

**Guiding actions:** *Foster lifelong learning and utilize your skills and talents.*

**Ask yourself:** *Does this celebrate my unique skills and gifts?*

## PRINCIPLE 3: THE HEART OF YOU—YOUR EMOTIONS ZONE

**Focus point:** This is your emotions, feelings, and self-awareness.

**Guiding action:** *Develop your best emotional intelligence.*

**Ask yourself:** *Do I take responsibility for my emotions, actions, and behavior?*

## PRINCIPLE 4: THE HUMANITY OF YOU— YOUR COMPASSION ZONE

**Focus point:** This is your role as a global citizen.

**Guiding action:** *Treat others with compassion.*

**Ask yourself:** *How does this impact others around me?*

## PRINCIPLE 5: THE SPORT OF YOU—YOUR WELLNESS ZONE

**Focus point:** This is your health and well-being.

**Guiding action:** *Champion lifelong well-being.*

**Ask yourself:** *Does this moment or action contribute to my longevity and well-being?*

## PRINCIPLE 6: THE SPIRIT OF YOU—YOUR HARMONY ZONE

**Focus point:** Cultivate harmony, inner peace, and contentment.

**Guiding action:** *Embrace harmony, inner peace, and being content.*

**Ask yourself:** *Is my mind at peace and my spirit content?*

These principles are another tool for your toolbox to help you discover about your life and choices. Also, on BestEverYou.com, we have multiple thought leaders who write about the principles in various articles and teachings each month, and Kris and I created a best-selling journal with videos for each prompt to go with the journal.

## SUCCESS TIP #13: Say Yes to Your Incredible Yes

One more amazing tool for you to use is called Incredible Yes. An

Incredible Yes is a moment where you said yes to someone or something and it changed your life. I believe we all have one, a few, or many Incredible Yes moments in us. When we interview people for *The Best Ever You Show* or for our summits, we ask people to share their Incredible Yes. One of my favorites is from Jack Canfield, who shared his experience of moving to California. He told us the story of how he moved from the Midwest to California, and it helped shape who he is today.

The biggest thing that happened in my life. I was living in Massachusetts. I took a training class—an insight training type of class with 350 people for a weekend type of training—and it really changed my life. The guy in charge asked me if I'd like to become a trainer for them and move to California. I said yes, which meant I'd have to sell the retreat center I owned and my home and land, which was around eleven acres in Massachusetts. Right as I was about to move, the guy rescinded the offer. Well, I had already sold my home, so my wife and I decided to move to California anyway. So we moved, and I started to meet all of these amazing people in this work I do called human development and personal growth. It was like the seedbed for all I do. Saying yes to a major move across country with no job opened up everything.

I shared an Incredible Yes moment similar to this. I had moved to California from Minnesota, and my Incredible Yes was then moving from California to Maine. Ahhh, Maine, what a beautiful place to be and call home for so many years now. I think about my life here and saying yes to moving here and now being able to say yes each day to my life rich with gratitude. Maine has a pace similar to where I grew up in Iowa. While I love huge cities, I find myself being much more at peace on a day-to-day basis with less commotion, more trees, fresh air, and a daily pace that has allowed both of us to base our careers from home since 2006.

An Incredible Yes could be a moment when someone says yes to you.

One of my more recent Incredible Yes moments through writing this book is meeting Dr. Harley Rotbart, who said yes to me. I asked him if he would share a story with our readers for this book, and it's one of my favorites. From that yes, other yes moments have happened, and we've come to know each other and become fast friends. We share a love for everything baseball, for example, and we support each other personally and professionally.

Dr. Rotbart has been a pediatric specialist for the past thirty-six years. He received his MD from Cornell University and was named one of the Best Doctors in America every year from 1996 through 2014, as well as receiving numerous other national awards for research, teaching, and clinical work. He developed and patented the gold-standard test for diagnosing viral meningitis, a test still used around the world today.

Dr. Rotbart is also a collector of miracles, which leads me to another success tip.

## SUCCESS TIP #14: Collect Miracles

Collect miracles wherever you can. Look for the extraordinary. As we move to this next story, it's evidence that miracles are possible.

## Stories from the Heart
### Harley A. Rotbart, MD—Collector of Miracles

I'm an evidence-based physician and scientist. I'm also a collector of miracles. Those may seem contradictory. They're not.

My "collection" began at a pivotal moment in my life, late one night during my pediatric residency training. I was working in the ICU at Children's Hospital of Philadelphia when two young brothers, ages three and seven, were brought in after near-drowning episodes. It was winter, and the three-year-old had fallen into a partially filled, icy swimming pool with enough residual water that he couldn't stand. His seven-year-old brother jumped in, pulled the younger boy to one of the pool's steps where the three-year-old's head was out of the water, but the seven-year-old was then himself overwhelmed by the freezing water and couldn't get out before submerging. When paramedics arrived, both boys were unconscious and not breathing. CPR was performed in the ambulance on the way to Children's Hospital.

In the ICU, the younger boy regained consciousness within a few hours and was neurologically normal. The older brother, our hero, remained in a coma for weeks.

The family stood vigil every day, and after our rounds and chores each evening, we, the residents, took over. We held the older boy's hand, talking and singing to him. It was on my watch late at night when I felt the seven-year-old squeeze my hand while I was reading to him. Just one squeeze. By that time, weeks into his stay in the ICU, discussions were beginning about brain death, discontinuing life support, and organ donation. I told everyone on rounds the next morning about the hand squeeze. Most of my colleagues and supervisors attributed it to an involuntary muscle spasm. Indeed, medically, by all our measures of brain function and assessments of neurologic recovery, there was not even the slightest possibility that this child made a conscious effort to squeeze my hand.

But then someone else also felt it after rounds the next morning, and then again that afternoon, now "on demand." The child's parents were overwhelmed with joy and hope when they felt their son's hand squeeze for the first time. None of us knew quite what to make of it or how much to hope for.

It would be several more days before the boy opened his eyes; a few hours after that he smiled, still with a breathing tube in place. When he walked out of the hospital more than two months after the near drowning and his heroic rescue of his little brother, we all cheered and cried. We had cried many times in the weeks preceding, and I still cry whenever I tell this story.

That was the first medical miracle in my career, and it has stuck with me for decades. Over the years, I would tell colleagues and trainees about that experience, and occasionally one of them would tell me of their own miraculous experience. Several years ago, while recovering from open-heart surgery, I wrote an essay about that long-ago experience with the little boy in the ICU. I sent the essay to physician colleagues and invited them to write to me about similar experiences they may have had. Many replied that they hadn't. But the remaining responses were most exciting for me. Those colleagues immediately replied with "Oh my goodness! I have an amazing story I've been waiting for the chance to tell." Not all of us are fortunate enough to encounter unexplained, unexpected, deeply moving, and mysterious moments in medicine. But when a medical miracle—physical, emotional, or both—does occur in a physician's career, it's unforgettable, in the forefront of our minds, and ripe for telling.

The essays from my colleagues moved me greatly. I edited them and compiled them into a book, *Miracles We Have Seen: America's Leading Physicians Share Stories They Can't Forget*. I donated all author proceeds from my miracles book to charities suggested by the physician-essayists. But the book was not the end of my "career" as a collector of miracles—it was just the beginning.

Albert Einstein said, "There are only two ways to live your life. One is as though nothing is a miracle. The other is as though everything is." Since my pivotal moment and that squeeze all those years ago, I'm in Einstein's second category—I see everything as a miracle. And you needn't be in a hospital or clinic to witness miracles. For me, miracles are objects and events in nature and in our lives that cannot be fully explained or re-created. Just look out a window and tell me how to explain *anything* you see. Can we really explain rain? Trees? Flowers? Can we create any of them from scratch? Hummingbirds are miraculous, aren't they, with the highest metabolic rate per body mass of any living animal and wings that beat up to eighty times per second. Per second! And how about bats? The saying "blind as a bat" belies their ability to feed on flying insects in total darkness by emitting sound waves and "hearing" the echoes of those waves on nearby insects—and then eating as many as 1,000 mosquitoes a night! Certain species of Monarch butterflies migrate 5,000 miles round trip each year, only to die shortly after their return—yet their *great*-grandchildren the next year (Monarchs have a short life span with several generations born in a year) take the identical route and even alight, en route, on the identical trees as their forebears. Not to be outdone, humpback whales also migrate more than 5,000 miles each year, from the cold waters where they feed to the warm waters where they give birth. Dolphins talk to one another, as do whales, but it turns out ants and gnats communicate as well. And what of the environment that supports these diverse species? Isn't our atmosphere a miracle, a perfect blend of gases that allow us to breathe while also allowing plants to breathe?

One final example—which will sound heretical in this era of pandemic. I even find viruses to be miraculous. Viruses have been the objects of my research for decades, and I've published dozens of medical and scientific papers about them. No one yet has created even a single virus from scratch. But when a single virus infects a cell, it can create one million more of itself in a matter of hours, shutting down the cell and, as we have so painfully learned recently from COVID-19, virtually shutting down all of human civilization! Miraculous.

And that's how an evidence-based physician and scientist can also be a collector of miracles. Indeed, the evidence for miracles is just outside our windows.

● ● ●

Now, the sort of medical and scientific miracles you've just read about are otherworldly and ethereal, delivered perhaps by a divine entity we can never see. They require a quiet examination of your own faith to believe, and therefore to behold. Nevertheless, they contain the sort of power that alters life trajectories, as does the miracle that is more tangible and, while also inked by faith, is delivered by another person.

Next, let's hear from Denise Zack, author, speaker, and mindfulness coach. See how a simple gesture can spark an inferno of goodwill, a miracle in its own right.

### Denise Zack, MS—Life's a Day at the Beach: Lessons in Mindfulness

It was a typical day at the beach. I spent the day with one of my good friends, laying in the sun, swimming in the ocean, and just enjoying the warm summer air. As the day turned into late afternoon, we thought we'd go for one more swim. The waves had become a little more turbulent and we thought we'd get one more good session of body surfing in before we called it quits and drove home. It was a decision that could've altered our lives forever. It certainly changed the course of events that day. As we swam out into the water preparing ourselves for body surfing, the sun tucked behind some clouds and the wind picked up. We didn't realize that, during all of our splashing, laughing, and looking for the "big one" that we could surf into shore, we had gone pretty far out.

The waves started picking up more, and before we knew it, they were coming in fast and furious, over our heads. The sea was angry and rough, and I knew that things had taken a turn for the worse. One particular wave towered over me, crashed on top of me, and pulled me under. Horrified, I realized that the undertow was pulling me out to sea. I kicked as hard as I could, reaching for the surface, until I was finally able to poke my head above the water and gasp for air. I looked around for my friend. She was nowhere in sight. Another wave came; the same thing. I kicked even harder this time, and as I finally pulled myself up, I turned around and saw my friend about 50 yards farther out to sea. It looked like she had given up. Her arms were flopped down by her sides as she got scooped up into a huge wave. I saw her mouth the word "help." I started to swim toward her, yelling her name, but another wave came and pushed me down again. I knew at that point I needed to go get help—I needed to get to shore.

I started kicking as hard as I could. I resolved that I wouldn't give up, telling myself, "I have strong legs, I'm a dancer, I can do this." And I kicked with all my might, swimming until I was almost all the way in.

It was then that I saw him—a figure coming from about twenty yards in front of me and to my left. He dove into the water and swam parallel to the shore under the water. He swam, I imagine with the undertow instead of against it, and miraculously made it to my friend who had gotten pulled way out behind me and to my right. He lifted her up over the waves and pushed her into shore with every surge of the water. In a few minutes, they both made it to shore, as did I. We were exhausted, still shaking, but so grateful that we made it in.

We were grateful for this young man who came out of nowhere to help us. We thanked him, and thanked him, and thanked him again. Words didn't seem to be enough. But we made a friend that day. And we stayed connected. The reason I tell you the story is twofold. The first reason is about mind-set. My friend and I were in similar circumstances, hers a little bit more intense than mine. But we had two different thought patterns going through our minds as I learned when we spoke afterward.

She was telling herself she was going to die, and I was telling myself I was going to make it.

When I looked back and saw her, she looked like she had given up. And I know that I didn't look that way. I kept fighting and pushing until I made it to shore.

Your reality is what you tell yourself. Your beliefs dictate your thoughts and emotions. Your beliefs dictate your assumptions and your expectations, and ultimately your energy and behavior. I told myself that I could get out of those waves, and I fought with everything I had. I was able to make it to shore. So, choose your words and your thoughts wisely. They can change—and sometimes save—your life.

The second reason I tell this story is about resources. We have many internal resources that we can call upon in difficult and challenging situations. Sometimes we forget that we have them. Sometimes they are automatic and leap into action at a moment's notice. And some of our resources come from outside. They can be material things like money or housing. They can be, and oftentimes are, people that we know who help us along the way.

Pay attention to what resources you have and use them. And pay attention to those that you need and don't be afraid to ask for help. Also, don't be afraid to accept help when someone offers it. I truly believe that people are put into our lives at certain times for very specific reasons. Don't be afraid to connect with people and allow them into your world. That is what strong and courageous people do. People think if they ask for help it's a sign of weakness. It's not. It's a sign of strength to be able to show vulnerability and let someone in who can support you.

That day, I used the resources I had: my strong mind, my strong body, and my will to live, and my friend took help from someone who was there at the right moment to help her in her hour of need. Both are what kept us alive that day and I am forever grateful.

● ● ●

I'm so grateful that Harley and Denise shared their messages of hope and discovery. Their stories remind us that anything is possible when you believe in yourself. Each moment is an opportunity to increase your impact and influence to elevate yourself and others around you to leave behind incredible footprints.

Keep going. You are right where you are supposed to be. Dig down deeper, reach more, and bury your feet in gratitude, self-love, self-worth, value, confidence, and more and don't give up.

As you proceed to Exercise 5, start to think about what moments you have had in your life that have been pivotal or changed your course.

## POINTS TO PONDER

Think. Write. Talk. Action. *(Because practice makes us our best.)*

### EXERCISE 5: Your Incredible Yes

Describe your Incredible Yes. This is a moment where you said yes to someone or something that then changed your life.

What is your Incredible Yes?

**1. Write your answer in your journal or below:**

_____

_____

**2. Describe another Incredible Yes:**

_____

_____

**3. If you don't have an Incredible Yes moment just yet, for what are you hoping and wishing?**

_____

_____

### EXERCISE 6: Tossing Spaghetti

Let's toss some spaghetti around.

**What are five crazy ideas you have?**

1. _____

2. _____

3. _____

4. _____

5. _____

Take one idea from above and write three additional ideas or goals you have for it.

Idea: _____

1. _____

2. _____

3. _____

Is it the best idea ever? Amazing. I sure hope so!

Is it in alignment with who you are and what you want to achieve in life?

Will it bring change in the world that you wish to see?

# CHAPTER 4
# GROW

*In the fourth point, we practice, refine, and redefine. As we practice these new steps with family, friends, and coworkers, we think, ponder, and focus on what produces positive results. We learn new things. We keep and expand what makes us be our best.*

**When you feel personally and** professionally empowered, you experience growth. Growth is a moment when you can look forward with perception, wisdom, and maturity—and look at the past without shame, blame, and regret. As you tossed spaghetti around in Chapter 3, you not only discovered; you also grew. You discovered more about yourself, and you now have an open mind.

## SUCCESS TIP #15: Your Success Has Deep Roots in Growth

Even creating this book, we tossed around some spaghetti as we chose the cover. Originally there were four choices. Then it came down to two. I printed them out and put the paper covers on other books to get a visualization. (It wasn't an easy decision as our design team is fabulous!) It was a really hard decision for me, and I asked for input from a lot of people. The winner in my eyes is the cover you see. I decided on it by writing down the feelings I had with each cover. This one was my choice because, to me, it best represents the growth I think we need as humanity, and I love the colors and vibe of it. I also loved the responses from other people. As our cousin Marie Osterman said, "It is dynamic and evokes change."

And that is the point. Change is dynamic. You know this because you know that exact feeling you have when you don't know something and you're going to have to go and grow through and wish XYZ to learn it. A freshman you send to college is different than the senior who returns. In fact, there is often huge growth when they come home for their first break after they've been away.

As you grow, you become wiser in every way. As a person, you practice, refine, and redefine. You may even age. You become wiser. In your wisdom, you learn that often in these moments you practice the fine art of forgiveness and applying love. You learn what brings you peace, joy, love, and more. As you practice these new steps with family, friends, coworkers, and others, you come to learn what produces positive results and moves you toward your vision and what doesn't.

## SUCCESS TIP #16: Keep and Expand What Helps You Be Your Best

When you feel stuck, you know it's time for growth. When you feel stuck with growth, it's important to remember that you are probably further along than you realize, and you still have more to learn. It's important to keep going and remember that you can't force the future. The future can't be rushed. The future is on a time clock, and you are on the clock. What you can have is an abundant mind-set with enough bliss to go around. You can understand what you are capable of and understand the kind of energy you want to attract.

As we let go of limiting beliefs, we become more aligned. As we think with our heart, we cultivate self-confidence and clarity. We may have sheer will and determination. We may have imagination and creativity. We may have an incredible work ethic and our best world-class mind-set and actions at the heart of it all.

So, in this point of change, what are you going to do? How will you sacrifice, grow, eliminate, and change to support your goals, values, beliefs, and dreams in alignment with your actions? Are you going to make a commitment for growth with your time and energy? Will that great idea just sit? Will your wishes come true? Are you taking action and growing, or are you perpetually contemplating?

Say this with me: "I welcome improvement." Now say this with me: "I invite improvement." Here is another: "I allow improvement." You can even add more to that sentence and be specific—for example, "I allow improvement in my health." Give yourself permission to grow. Give yourself permission to do something else and explore your success.

Are you feeling empowered? Do you know your value? Do you remember your value?

●　●　●

Sometimes we block our own success because we have allowed someone to make us feel less than valued, perhaps even worthless. I've been on conference calls, for example, discussing pricing for services, and it's one of the biggest concerns people get stuck on: What should I charge?

I'll ask, "What is your service worth?"

"I don't know," they respond.

I'll say, "Do you feel valued?"

They respond, "I don't know what that means. What does that mean?"

I'll politely explain, and together we'll visit the land of vision statements about value and worth.

The answer is rooted in worth, self-worth, self-love, time, energy, and love. It *all* goes to value. The questions to ask yourself again and again until you know the answers are as follows:

- What would make you feel more valued?
- Do you have people around you who value you?
- Are you loved?
- Do you feel loveable?
- Do you know your self-worth?
- Do you practice self-care?

As you explore growth and success, the people who are in your everyday life and moments matter. You may need a fine-tuning in the relationships department for your best, most successful self. I say surround yourself with love. It's a fact that sometimes we outgrow others, family included. We grow to that point where we stand firmly in our choices.

For example, a client of mine had recently gone dairy free, and someone presented with an offer of ice cream. She politely declined. When the next person pressed her to come back over to their dairy life, she again politely declined and added, "No, thank you. I've gone dairy free." Then they poked again and said, "That's nonsense. It's a total fad." My client sticks to her convictions and her new method of operation.

I'll try as hard as I can on this next point to be positive, but *wow!*— being around those who know the old me and sticking to my new choices can be super challenging. Being around those who have different behaviors can be a big challenge, too.

You've changed and they haven't, or they haven't accepted the fact that you have or disagree with you or whatever is going on. You've been in their box and they've been in with you—and now you are outside their comfort zone, and they are faced with adapting or not.

Same goes for any change that is forced upon you. You have a choice. Adapt or not. Things may not go according to that plan, but what if things will all work out? What if all your hard work pays off in other ways? What would happen if you assumed that a positive outcome would take place?

So yes, people around you block growth in various ways. But sometimes you block your own success as well, as my pretzel theory explains.

## SUCCESS TIP #17: Learn Elizabeth's Pretzel Theory

You ready for my pretzel theory?

(Okay, so please don't really do this exercise as it is completely ridiculous. Just go with it and consider making it even more crazy to illustrate my point with me.)

**Step 1: Take your right leg and place it behind your left ear.**

**Step 2: Now take your left leg and place it behind your right ear.**

**Step 3: Take your right hand and grab your left shoulder.**

**Step 4: Take your left hand and grab your right shoulder.**

Voila! You are now a delicious pretzel ready for consumption, and guess what? As my theory goes, if you twist yourself into a pretzel to please others, you'll be eaten alive.

Kris Fuller and Quaid Guarino have tested this pretzel configuration, so we know for sure it works. Quaid, bless his heart, got down on the carpet in my office and actually had both feet by his ears. I was laughing so hard. He's saying, "Oh, Mom, you totally got me." It was super funny. Again, don't really do this pretzel exercise, but do know the theory because chances are—at some point or maybe consistently—you have molded and twisted and turned yourself in your lifetime into many a new pretzel shape to please others.

## SUCCESS TIP #18: When You Stop Inventing New Pretzel Shapes to Morph into, Then You Truly Grow as a Person

I mean, I'm all in for a bag of the best Unique Extra Dark Splits money can buy. After all, these are my husband's favorites, but if you don't want that bag of pretzels consumed, we must do things like practice forgiveness, set some healthy and clear boundaries, apply love, and live with no regrets. I write this as my husband just opened a bag, and he loved what I wrote.

The people around you are growth amplifiers or growth inhibitors. The folks around you who twist and tie you into people-pleasing pretzels are complete growth prohibitors.

Another realm that either fosters or stalls our growth is not knowing how to forgive others or ourselves. Inner peace is a benefit of forgiveness. Forgiveness is twofold: forgiveness of others and also forgiving ourselves, so that we live our lives with no blame, shame, or regrets. People tell you that it's important to practice no-regrets living. If we aren't careful and we don't live life with forgiveness, we may head to the laundry list of regrets, shame, and blame we have and live there.

It's not that easy to just go around and do what someone tells us to do. I'm thinking of a taking-out-the-garbage analogy here, and maybe that is exactly what we need to do: take out the garbage, so to speak, and clear our minds of the negativity by practicing forgiveness. It still might be easier said than done sometimes, right? When you ask someone to take out the garbage, they either do so willingly or they stomp around and totally hate the chore. It depends on how stinky the garbage is in our house. But either way, it's another common change that people generally don't love doing, especially at 6:30 in the morning in winter here in Maine. And if you forget to take out the garbage, well, in some cases you may not hear the end of that mistake for hours or days if the garbage has to wait a week. Talk about needing forgiveness, especially if the garbage is totally gross. Might have a momentary regret!

Personally, I've been busy working on forgiving myself for the moments surrounding my dad passing away. I had talked to him and I have voice-mails recorded on my phone, so I don't have regrets. I have more of a regret for the way he passed away, as there was no longer any hope in the matter. I am an optimist when it comes to health and people surviving. I'm right there cheerleading and helping along whoever it is to get well, including myself if need be. But that wasn't this situation. He was not coming home, and we all knew it. Minnesotans have a new river that I cried for them. My dad had been in and out of multiple hospitals in 2018. In late 2018, he had multiple medications and lifesaving measures necessary to keep him alive. It was hopeless, which frustrated me so much. We were out of miracles for our ICU warrior, and this time no sweaters from Kohl's turned into super-hero capes were going to work.

I was recalling this with my sister Alex, whom I told you about in an earlier chapter. She's the one who will tell you that it was especially difficult as she had their new baby girl on one floor while my dad came in through the emergency and was on another. My mom said it was just awful going back and forth from the ICU floor to the maternity floor.

The whole experience for me was traumatic. As I chatted with Alex for this book, she said, "You know, we all process things differently, and there are a lot of family members. Even as you write this, someone will recall it a different way or have their spin. We all process events and grief in different ways." Wise words from my sister as she was chatting with me on Zoom, showing me her newest addition to our family: another baby girl, who by the way is so perfect.

For many months after my dad died, I proceeded to beat myself up silently and nearly hated myself for not doing more. At this time, my self-care plummeted. I kept replaying seeing him take his last breath and won-dering and wishing, which in hindsight was futile. I was there and heard the doctors and I understood intellectually what was taking place. But some-thing else happened to me on a heart level. Upon returning home, the world really didn't make sense. I was beyond brokenhearted, completely devas-tated, and felt utterly lost. I'm told this happens to people when a loved one passes. It makes you realize with more perspective that nearly everything in life is small, trivial, and not as important as you think. People don't seem to understand that many things just aren't worth arguing over or worrying about. In this personal existential crisis, I used a tad too much food and my favorite comfy couch to figure it out. So, for all of 2019 and much of 2020, I studied forgiveness and began to ease up on myself. Moments were and still are really different without my dad around. He was an amazing man whom I loved with my whole heart.

Well, enter Dr. Harley Rotbart on my radio and TV show, and it was like he completely understood and could relate to my dad stories, baseball, and my life. I think I could write a sentence, any sentence, and he could finish it. He's just absolutely wonderful, as you know from his story. Through reading his books and meeting him, I have a much better understanding of forgiveness and the incredible importance of it, especially with respect to living your life with no regrets, which also happens to be the title of one of my all-time favorite books by Dr. Rotbart. Here is one of my favorite quotes from his book:

> Growth requires moving on from the past, including from any regrets you might have, forgiving yourself if necessary . . . and recognizing all the good you've done in your life and all you have to be proud of. Take a step back and take the time to recognize your growth and evolution so far, marvel at how different, how much more mature and wiser, your perspectives are now than they were when you were younger. The changes speak to your willingness to learn and to develop the prepared mind.

This next one's dedicated to you, Harley.

## SUCCESS TIP #19: Practice Forgiveness for Yourself and for Others So That You Live Life with No Regrets

So how do we forgive ourselves for real? What is the action you need to take? There are many, and here is one of my favorites. More appear in the exercises at the end of this chapter.

For now, say this: I *am* now at peace with _____ [name of person].

When you say that, don't add any qualifiers or other information.

The action is to get quiet and then get quieter. Listen, watch, grow, and become.

Often when we don't forgive, we get loud, louder, and angry even. We may avoid the topic or the person, say bad things, or swear. And I get it; sometimes it feels better, but that still isn't true forgiveness. So, I'd like to challenge you to become more powerful internally without being externally loud. I'd like to also suggest that you don't need to be loud and you don't have to muster up energy to become a complete badass to grow and change. In fact, when I was growing up, being a "bad ass" meant more like a horse's ass and you were in constant detention, causing trouble and annoyance.

One of the best growth moments there is, is to just be *you*. Be your Best Ever You in this moment in time. You know what you know, and you'll grow what you grow. You'll forgive when you are ready, and hopefully that is sooner rather than later. You might need to gain more confidence or get support to accomplish things or learn more, but you certainly don't need to be a bitch or an a$$hole, tell everyone to go fly a kite, or do a 180 personality-wise to get what you need done, to make your point, or to avoid forgiveness. Forgiveness isn't about the other person. It's about how you internally process it and your own health. When you hold on to not forgiving others, you are only hurting yourself. The other people most likely have no clue.

You don't need to proclaim your forgiveness to anyone but yourself, even if you are forgiving someone else. Most likely what the world just needs is more of *you*. Be confidently *you*—with your smile, your attention, your caring, your talents, and the lives you touch person by person with grace, gratitude, compassion, and collaboration.

*Grow!* Grow as a person. Grow to listen and observe and pause for forgiveness.

As you grow, you may realize that your life needs more editing. That's okay. What do you do when this happens? You're going to grow more and change more by being here with me. You'll be able to better recognize how to utilize change methods to find and renew or reconnect with success.

Sometimes we are in reconnect or recovery mode. I use the term "drift" probably more than I should, but what I mean is when we've moved away from our connection with ourselves and need to reconnect. We may need to reengage with our authentic, truest self. A drift moves us away from our goals and our authentic self. Drifts can occur for many reasons, but I think the main culprits are comfort and laziness; multiple other internal or external reasons are often at play also.

My drift happened after my dad died when I decided for the second time in my life to stop feeling sorry for myself. The first time I decided this was back in 2005 when my dad was in a rehab facility recovering from a devastating stroke. He recited the entire alphabet using powerful motivation words like benevolence, courage, and determination when no one thought his speech ability was even intact. I decided in that moment that if he could do it, so could I, and I stopped feeling sorry for myself that I had life-threatening food allergies. It's why I coined the phrase "the drift" to explain the process of becoming unrecognizable to myself and maybe even to others. In the second instance, as I explained, I had packed on way too many pounds since 2018 and stopped most exercise. I wasn't unhappy, but I was not paying attention at all to myself. I had drifted from much of what I value, which is being athletic, eating carefully, being well, and making time to do silly, goofy things. The biggest thing that I am working on forgiving myself for is that I had pretty much stopped writing and wasn't going to dare put my face on a video in the age of social media everything.

What a drifting (and overeating) soul I had become. As I was learning to forgive, my pants were not forgiving me. Then I decided to make peace with myself.

I got a new phrase in my head.

## SUCCESS TIP #20: Grow So Much You Find Peace

This phrase confused me at first and even made me giggle. I said, "Yup, I've grown so much here, this isn't peaceful." But then my pizza monster self quieted down and started to forgive myself. For everything. I systematically went through my life and patted myself on my back and said, "You knew what you knew at the time. I forgive you. Relax and go forward. You know better now."

But I could still hear the pepperoni pizza, like a choir, calling me by my first name. I had to forgive my drift and reconnect with my truest self and fire up the green smoothie machine, once again.

In times like these, you need to find some pivot points. Find adjustments you can make, especially in those moments when you've experienced the growth before or you are down on your luck or self and you must keep going and adjust even more. It's a moment to resolutely reevaluate, while standing firmly in choices or changing again. You can choose to start new things, and stop some and continue others. You can choose pros and cons even, which can be a great assist. Additionally, I love a solid R word of choice as the center of my power.

When you need to revise your life, the R words are here for you.

Often we just need subtle, refining adjustments to remind ourselves of the beauty in our choices. You choose, in each moment, how to punctuate your life. Many of us are searching for what inspires us. It can be difficult to sustain the momentum of inspiration and necessary to seek it. One of the best ways to find inspiration is with a family of R words that involve becoming unstuck or are associated with change. Here are a few of my favorites:

| | | |
|---|---|---|
| Reset | React | Retake |
| Revise | Redo | Retry |
| Revoke | Resilient | Relearn |
| Reality | Re-create | |

In your journal or below, write down five words that start with R that resonate with you:

1. _____     4. _____
2. _____     5. _____
3. _____

And yet, still the best growth word isn't really an R word at all. It's actually the F word: *forgiveness*. Forgiveness is empowering and fosters inner peace.

Pivot points, adjustments, growth and adjusting to growth, reevaluating, standing firm with values and choices, making best decisions, learning and practicing forgiveness, setting boundaries—these are your tools for change.

# Stories from the Heart
## Paul, My Relationship with Change

I have a very interesting relationship with Change. We met as early as I can remember, and my first impression was not favorable. To be truthful, Change probably didn't like me very much either. To be even more truthful, the reason our relationship didn't find success until recently was because of my immaturity and stubbornness—the same reason my relationship with my older sister didn't blossom until late, but I digress.

The first time I remember meeting Change was in the late 1990s on a rainy, thunderous night in New England. It was particularly scary. I was trying to unlatch a deadbolt lock. My mom was on the other side of the door, crying. My dad, who was inside with me, had his lenses and frames in his hand. I'm not sure if it was the hysterics of the crying or the weather that was more unsettling, but I started crying. My mom was practically begging me to open the door. I was four or five years old. This was the beginning of a serious change in my life.

I would spend the next decade of my life as a defense attorney for two clients: Mom and Dad. I would represent my father against my mother, and my mother against my father. Pro bono, naturally. A pretty daunting task for someone who was trying to figure out how to tie their shoes and spell their own name.

I moved schools what seemed like every other year and things behind the scenes were not going swimmingly. I wore masks, so you would never know, but it was tough. There is a pretty extensive history of alcohol and drug abuse on both sides of my family, and, to an extent, violence as well. It is fair to say that these three ingredients made up a good majority of my childhood: drugs, alcohol, and violence.

I played Little League, too, so it wasn't *all* bad. There was a dinner-at-the-table stretch of time for a while, but it didn't last. It wasn't sustainable. One night, it got so bad ("so bad" could be defined as a physical altercation between parents, a physical altercation between my parents and me, police being called, things being thrown, things being said, parents being under the influence, uncovering drugs, etc.), I actually packed a bag and jumped out of my own (first-floor) window, and fled home. Change. Again.

My school attendance was always really good (besides a couple stretches in high school that I cover). I rarely, if ever, missed school. School was a place for me, at times, to take my mask off! It was refreshing. But sometimes (often) I got into trouble. It was usually pretty harmless. A handful of times I found myself in a situation where it would have been, as my dad says, "Easier to stay out of, than to get out of."

For the early part of my life, it was survive-and-advance mode. As a child, my objectives were really just try and be a kid as much as I could. Unfortunately, the dynamics between my parents wouldn't really allow that, so I had to embrace that reality—even though I didn't realize at the time that is what I was doing. After I ran away from home, I ended up with Dad. At the time, he was living in New England, so I enrolled at a local school. Within two years, Dad decided it would be best to move across the country. Thirty-two hundred ground miles later we settled in a new place. It wasn't long before we were on our way *back* home to where we moved from. Change.

Once resettled, the results of my own choices came back to bite me. I was given an ultimatum by my dad: "Quit makin' these choices, or go and live with your mother [and stepdad]." Immature and stubborn, I chose the latter. More Change. At this point of our relationship, Change and I are not on the same page. In fact, I have come to resent Change altogether. I was pretty withdrawn from my new surroundings. I started smoking pot as a sophomore and got into a pretty serious depression. I would find ways to convince my mom to let me stay home from school. At one point, I was trying to find a way to transfer schools. It got pretty bad.

I can still remember two days in particular.

The first is the day that my relationship with my big sister shifted forever. The second is the day that my relationship with Change shifted forever. The first was when I asked my sister if I could spend the night in her room because I was pretty shaken by an altercation that had happened between our mom and stepdad. This was during my middle school years. Of course she said yes. We watched *Legally Blonde*. I just remember opening up and asking for help and getting exactly what I needed (and more) from my big sister in that moment.

The second was when I actually had to leave a class in high school because I was so upset. I had been getting teased by a classmate (who is actually now one of my dearest friends: W.B.). After I left class, I went to an empty part of the building. I sat on the floor, distraught. Someone walked by and introduced themself and invited me to a party at their house: my first official high school party invite. I ended up not going. But it was this extension of friendship that allowed me to show up to school the next day. And the day after that. Eventually, I tried out for the basketball team, and the following year ran for student council. Both of these instances were momentous for me because they taught me invaluable lessons. The first was that it is okay, and oftentimes necessary to lean on and ask for support. The second is that the way the world perceives you, the way you perceive yourself, and the way you want to be perceived are three completely different things. In the moment when I was getting teased, I thought I was the lamest person in the world and that I was completely alone and isolated. I also had never really considered the fact that I actually had control over a lot more of my situation than I thought. Once I leaned into Change and got to know Change a little bit, I started to see a shift.

This shift allowed me to start to see a future for myself. This future included helping people navigate their own unique challenges and circumstances through teaching and coaching. It was important for me to realize: *Everywhere I go, there I am.* In other words, if I kept moving from school to school (whether it was within my control or not), it was important for me to understand that if I didn't modify my choices and behavior, I would see the same results. There were some things that were out of my control, but I also had a lot of control of things, such as how to treat people, how to be dependable, how to bring and spread kindness and joy, and how to encourage. The tricky part is embracing seemingly scary, hard, or insurmountable Change, without having tangible evidence or results to do so. I liken it to being a great singles player in tennis. You cannot hit great shots without having great confidence, but you cannot have great confidence without hitting great shots, so where do you begin? You begin with surrounding yourself with great support, and you lean on that support. Ask for help. Lean on support. Ask for more help.

We all have unique obstacles in our lives that we need to overcome or be overcome by. I think for me the important thing to consider is that you are not necessarily getting to a place of arrival. People often say things like "Once I get this job I'll be all set," or "Once the kids turn eighteen we'll be great," or "Once this semester is over it'll be good." And some of that may be true. But Change is inevitable in all our lives. Like the relative who just stops over unannounced, and you may get really anxious because the house is a mess (even though it really isn't *that* bad). It is better to *stay* ready for Change than it is to *get* ready for Change. I don't feel like I've pulled myself through; I feel like I am *pulling* myself through. It is an ongoing process in which I need to be an active participant. How we work *with* (or against) Change will ultimately be up to each of us.

Today, I am a teacher and coach. I feel incredibly fortunate and motivated to show up to school and practice each day with an opportunity to work with students, athletes, and colleagues. I pride myself on taking things in stride and being someone who has a really positive relationship with Change. Having overcome a lot of adverse experiences both on my own and with the help of others, I take a tremendous amount of responsibility and pride in being able to instill confidence in those around me to do the same for themselves, and to also support them through their own experiences.

Paul's story inspires us to learn more about growth through change and visualizing the future beyond current circumstances. Next, Fiona shares a story of grace and tenacity and the ability to see her vision for herself with clarity at a young age.

## Fiona Joy Hawkins—To Live with Grace

As a child I was a chronic dreamer. I spent my life staring out the window playing the A movie, the one where I'm doing a concert in the Sydney Opera House, winning an award, or watching a movie when one of my songs comes on. I lived in that shadowy place between dreamland and the impossible, and yet I hoped my dreams would come true one day.

Born to teenage parents in a small mining town in New South Wales, Australia, I was introduced to the piano at age eight when my grandmother moved in with an old German iron-frame. I fell in love with it and from that moment forth wanted to be a concert pianist and composer when I grew up.

At the same age I was diagnosed with Tourette syndrome (TS). Sometimes our weakness gives us strength. TS taught me lots of things about people and toughened me up. Having obvious twitches also meant I knew how to stay away from scrutiny. I spent much of my childhood avoiding being looked at by sitting at the back of the classroom, and yet I ended up as an adult right in front of everyone's focus on the stage and under lights! It was a strange twist of fate.

No one noticed tics when I played the piano. I hid them within the music, and this translated as a musical dance. I had a sense of belonging when I played and knew I wanted music in my life more than anything. The piano was my gift, my superpower, and my saving grace.

As a child I believed anything was possible and didn't realize someone could stand in the way of my musical dreams. Success is not just about finding what sets your soul on fire, or the things you are good at. It's about making sure that no one takes them away from you.

Immature, naïve, and sheltered, I married at nineteen.

Shortly after, we moved to San Francisco. It was right at the time when George Winston and Windham Hill became a worldwide phenomenon. I turned the radio on one day and had an instant sense of belonging. The music I was writing had a name: New Age music. It was a lightbulb moment.

After a few years of living in various countries, we returned home to Australia but there was something missing. I was living my husband's life and career, and the future didn't seem to hold any chance for me to change that. Being discouraged and unable to explore my musical potential left me feeling trapped and without the ability to explore my worth.

We had two lovely children along the way, and though I tried hard to make a perfect world for them (despite some difficulties), I felt I failed them as well as myself.

The piano kept calling to me, and deep down I knew it held the key to my future. Something was absent and I had to find it.

After a twenty-five-year marriage that stopped me from living my best life and being my best self, it was time to find some missing courage and make a life-altering decision. That day arrived one bright sunny morning in September 2008.

There are negatives and positives in leaving one world and stepping into another, and no one tells us how these decisions may play out. I realized I wouldn't discover the answer until I made the leap, gained a sense of self, and decided to explore the very things that drive me: creativity and music.

My mother advised me that no child will look back and say thanks to a parent for staying in an unsuitable marriage or in a place where you are not happy, and that I would not be teaching my children anything by sticking with the marriage for their sake. She said they learn by watching the decisions you make and the reasons you make them, and basics like self-fulfillment and happiness are worthy reasons.

I wish more people had explained my personal rights to happiness, a career, and love, the need to be honest with myself, and that it's okay to move on when things are not right—but mostly, that it's okay to want for yourself. I had been married to a controlling man, so the decision to make my own choices and owning the mistake to stay so long was empowering.

When two people do the dance of divorce, no one person should be blamed. I remember telling a friend my tale of woe, and he said something that stopped me in my tracks. "You talk as if it's all his fault, but you were there, and you allowed it to happen because you stayed." They weren't words I wanted to hear, but they were wise and true. I needed to own my problems and fix them myself.

It took eighteen months to work through the twists and turns of disentanglement, but nine years later I have a career, I'm in a safe place, and I have learned more about life and myself than I imagined. I remarried and discovered you can find love and have your own identity at the same time.

We all have a purpose and things of value to share. Following that pathway is essential to happiness, but to find it we need freedom mixed with a sprinkling of self-belief. Learning to stand up for yourself is a hard lesson and possibly the catalyst for my reset decision. It changed my life in so many ways. It allowed me to move forward and yet it took me right back to where I started: the piano.

My career has taken me many places, but one of my favorites is buried in the lyrics of my song "Grace":

"To be with Grace, to live with Grace, always with Grace."

[The song "Grace" by Fiona Joy Hawkins is on *Winds of Samsara* (Ricky Kej and Wouter Kellerman), which went on to win a Grammy for Best New Age Album in 2015.]

I'm grateful to Paul and Fiona for sharing their personal stories with us. They are both very inspiring for finding strength and growth under multiple difficult circumstances. What did you learn from their stories? What are some important growth points you've had in your life? As we move on to Exercises 7 and 8, remember to anchor in your power.

In Exercise 7, we are going to go through some forgiveness exercises. In Exercise 8, we are going to become our empowered best selves. If you need assistance, please reach out and I'll be happy to help you.

## POINTS TO PONDER

**Think. Write. Talk. Action.** *(Because practice makes us our best.)*

### EXERCISE 7: What Forgiveness Sounds, Looks, and Feels Like

Who are you ready to forgive?

Complete these sentences and read them out loud:

1. I *am* now at peace with _____ [name of person].

2. I *am* now at peace with _____ [name of person].

3. I *am* now at peace with _____ [name of person].

Next, write a letter of forgiveness to one of the three people you just listed. This is for you, not them, so don't feel a need to send it. Next, repeat each of the sentences above, out loud, ten times. Shout them if you need to. If you need an accountability partner in forgiveness, give me a call. Forgiveness is one of my favorite topics, and I believe a huge chunk of what it takes to bring internal, lasting peace and success in all areas of your life.

Now here is the million-dollar question: Did you forgive yourself? If you were busy writing in other people's names, beautiful. Next, let's forgive ourselves.

*I am now at peace with* _____ [your name].

Say that ten or twenty or thirty times. It is time to ease up on yourself, forgive yourself for whatever you need to be at peace with, and move forward in your moments-matter fashion.

### EXERCISE 8: Your Empowered Best You

Take a look at what you wrote in Exercise 3.

In a journal or below, write down three areas on which you would like to continue to work.

1. **Area of focus:** _____

Statement of empowerment: _____

Goal 1: _____

Goal 2: _____

2. Area of focus: _____

Statement of empowerment: _____

Goal 1: _____

Goal 2: _____

3. Area of focus: _____

Statement of empowerment: _____

Goal 1: _____

Goal 2: _____

## REFLECTION POINT

What does success sound like? What will you hear?

_____

What does success look like? What will you see?

_____

What does success feel like? What will you feel?

_____

## EMPOWERMENT AND LETTING GO

Are you ready to let go of any habits or behaviors? People?

_____

**Here is another empowering sentence. Complete three statements of letting go.**

Because I *am* empowered to be my best, I *am* now able to let go of

_____

Because I *am* empowered to be my best, I *am* now able to let go of

_____

Because I *am* empowered to be my best, I *am* now able to let go of

_____

# PART 2

# ALIGN YOUR TRUTHS

# CHAPTER 5
# SUPPORT

*At point 5 we seek support. This can be learning to help ourselves or a moment to ask for outside assistance. When we overcome or heal, we seek support internally or externally. This is a moment where we ask for help from others, seek professional help, heal, and realize we are not alone. This often serves as a huge, pivotal moment for people in how we move from being stuck to taking action, and taking the right actions, so we don't fall back on old habits and patterns that don't serve us well. With support comes feedback. Our new selves may need to reach out for feedback. We may give ourselves permission to ask those with whom we interact for feedback and redefine if necessary. We may or may not incorporate this feedback based on how it makes us feel to the core. Support can be difficult, as we may or may not want insights that don't let us stay comfortable.*

**Of all the points of change,** this seems to be the one that really gets people to squirm. It can be very difficult to say, "I need help," and admit it to yourself or to others.

## SUCCESS TIP #21: Ask for Help when You Need It

Ask for help when you need it, especially if it's financial, medical, emotional, or with an addiction or so many other things. People, for whatever reason, equate the words "I need help" with "I've failed" or "I suck" or "I'm less than" or "I don't know what I am doing" or whatever negative energy vibration you want to use in a sentence that indicates or makes you feel like you don't have a clue what is going on—or at least you think someone is going to perceive that, judge you, or think negatively about you, or worse, let the cat out of the bag and tell someone else.

There are multiple meanings to the words "I need help." It could be you are world class and already plenty and you need to move to your next title. It really could mean a full-on mayday rescue call with all systems having failed and you are asking for help. But here is what we forget in these moments. First, we all have them. Second, we all have them, and third, yes, we all have them. From changing that flat tire to staying after class for extra help to that awesome coach who taught you a new pitch to the people you call to run by all chapters of a book once or twice, we all need support whether we admit it or not.

Here is what we also forget. We love to feel needed.

## SUCCESS TIP #22: Allow People to Help You

People love to feel needed. We love to lend a hand, lend our expertise, and oh my gosh, we love to dish out advice to those who will listen.

## SUCCESS TIP #23: Filter the Advice That Comes with Help

Seriously, people will tell you till the cows come home everything they think you should be doing. Opinions from others must go through your filtration system. When someone offers up their unsolicited opinion, give them a lot of thanks and send it right on over to YPFS (Your Personal

Filtration System). Here we decide what gets recycled into the universe and what is kept with us. Advice goes back into those six questions you can ask yourself or look into your heart to see if it resonates—and if it does, great; if it doesn't, so be it. But sound the alarm when someone says, "You really should . . . ," because advice is coming through your ears and into your brain, heart, energy, and soul, and if you don't have the filtration system on, it could spell trouble. Pause and filter with all advice, solicited or otherwise.

Align advice to what is true for you. As we talk about support and the next few points of change, we align with our truth and keep in mind that a greater world out there needs our support and help. Each person is a give-and-take, and if you listen carefully, humanity needs us all right now. It is our responsibility to help one another. *All* of us, all around the world. We all are intertwined and interconnected, and we all have a responsibility to one another. It is here where we ask for help in an effort to achieve, overcome, get through, sometimes, succeed—more individually and collectively.

Often, we must pause again and pay attention to the world around us to see another's truth. Skip past the surface and without judgment; there are moments when another struggle is real and showing up right in front of your eyes. Do you keep to yourself? Do you get out your phone to record or observe? Do you help?

Several times in the past few years, I've been in back of women in a grocery store line who were struggling for grocery money with at least one small child in the cart. They didn't ask me for help. I gave it anyway and paid for the groceries. I didn't say a word, didn't make a production out of it, and I'm only telling you here so that you remember to stop and pay attention to those not asking for help who clearly need it. Give it. Your kindness changes their moment and perhaps even their trajectory.

Asking for support and lending support goes both ways. The moments wax and wane. I think about being in the hospital during my worst allergic reaction and the help I received. I think about the trucker who stopped to pick up my brother Justin roadside after he had been the victim of one of the most heinous crimes in the state of Minnesota. I think of the time one of our son's friends stayed with us for months as his sister rehabbed from a terrible accident. She is now in the Paralympics. I think about so many instances in our family where we have been helped or helped another.

This is a moment where we may reach within to help ourselves as our key resource, or we may seek professional help. Again remember, when I say "seek professional help," it may resonate with you in such a way that I'm suggesting something is wrong or that you must heal and learn. It doesn't have to be heard that way. Remember, professional help is all over the map. It could be a coach you hire to win the Olympics. It might be a therapist you hire to help heal your past. It might be a person you hire to bake a cake for your wedding. "Seek professional help" doesn't necessarily mean something is wrong. You might seek professional help that propels you on your way to even more greatness.

Either way, this can be a huge pivotal moment for you in how you move from being stuck to taking action and taking the right actions, so you don't fall back on old habits and patterns that don't serve you well or get you where you want to be.

On our soul-seeking adventure within this book, this is a moment where, with perhaps an outside look in, you embrace your space and perhaps even see your perceived faults as gifts and amplify your authenticity in every area of your life. Remember, you hold your power.

Remember, "I need help" is perhaps one of the hardest phrases for people to dare utter, aside from "I'm sorry" and "I was wrong." These can be especially tricky if you were raised under the air of not letting the outside world know anything is wrong and putting on that happy face for all to see. Meanwhile, all hell could be breaking loose in the background and the outside world; perhaps even a neighbor or close friend would be stunned to hear what was really happening.

This past winter, my husband received a call for help from a friend. This friend had fallen in his garage so badly he couldn't move. My husband

and one of our sons, Quinn, rushed over to help him and ensure his safety. That's one type of support. Situation remedied, and we moved on. This is probably the most common kind of support. Help me move, help me with this task or another. We're there in a shot, task complete.

Support has many faces and names, however, and some moments aren't so easily solved and the situation at play may be life-altering. They don't necessarily need to have been life-threatening, either, but often are. From a move across country to help to reach a vision you have for yourself, support is, for many, full of aha moments when change is really allowed to happen because your A-team is assisting you.

I do not think we achieve without support: support combined with teaching about supporting others and contributing to your immediate surroundings.

Even as I write this, I am sitting in my chair and just pulled away from my keyboard for some moments to reflect and to really think about what to say next. In writing this, I've had so many moments of needing to ask for support and also in turn have been asked to help out. I'm thinking of the people I've personally turned to now and during my life as a whole who have helped me become unstuck or move forward. I love help from others, and I also love to help others in return.

How about you? Are you in a position where you need to ask for help? Are you in a position where you are helping someone else? Are you doing both for various things?

Be brave. Live and show up authentically. You are loved. Be you. Ask for help or give help to others who need you in that moment.

When you think of support, collaborations, or the team you put together, carefully place who is closest to you with intention, which can include family. These are your influencers. This is especially true if you have huge, lofty goals that you are dreaming about, but no lofty goal support crew who has already been down the flight path to show you how to navigate.

● ● ●

I coached a woman recently who shared that she is from a family of alcoholics and her family members abuse antidepressant medications. Her goal in working with me was to achieve well-being. As we unpacked her box, I learned that she feared becoming like her family and was reaching for new information so that she had the support she needed to continue to be a nondrinker and do everything in her power to overcome her situation and to change her life so that antidepressants were not something she ate as part of her daily diet of well-being. Her surrounding influencers' behaviors offered key information to help her help herself and seek additional support as she became more aware of how her past was carrying her forward. Being a lifelong nondrinker myself, I feel comfortable knowing that flight path of success, so I shared my experiences as we moved forward together. She had a feeling that we were meant to know each other, and my experiences served to reinforce what she already knew but needed extra support, validation, and reassurance in those moments.

When you think about asking for support, think about this: A person aspiring to be a professional baseball player isn't going to seek a mentor in the airline industry. That would be silly. Instead, a kid with dreams of making the Big leagues is going to be best served by the coach who signed on the dotted line and perhaps won the World Series.

This goes for advice, too. We all need support. We all need to give support to others.

In 2020, when I met Kris Fuller, I told her I needed help and I needed to refuel from what had happened in 2018–2019, and I just still didn't feel my Best Ever Me. Well, as it turns out, I needed more help with grief than I thought. Up to the moment I met Kris, days before our beloved dog passed away and then before, I was still decently shaken up from my dad passing away in October 2018. There was just a lot going on already when my grieving mom needed her own life-altering surgery weeks before my fiftieth birthday in September 2019.

I was feeling like I needed a break to turn inward to heal. It happens.

Life was choppy, like a rough sea with waves crashing in from all directions. It felt a bit like I was on a big, tall wave and then sucked under trying to tread water. Then Kris threw the life preserver out, and I'm glad that thing was big enough for the two of us because what happened next made it feel like we needed a whole rescue team.

I remember being on a video call with Kris and saying to her, "Is that Ben? He looks like he's lost so much weight." I was going at this from happiness for Ben and "What diet is that?" and I-want-to-know-about-this mode. Kris shares her story in one of the chapters to come, but the stage 4 colon cancer diagnosis was not what any of us expected. My beautiful, sweet friend, in all her positive energy and faith and hope—I knew in my heart she was going to lose her husband and it was only a matter of when. So there we are and were, both navigating. We decided to place as much positive energy into the universe as possible to heal me and prepare Kris for what appeared to be the inevitable.

And so, knowing the moments that were going to follow, we knew we needed to support each other, which included at some level feeling useful and being productive and maybe even at times being distracted during moments of despair. We examined our Best Ever You founding principles and applied them to our lives. We also wrote a journal and did fifty-two video prompts to accompany the journal. We laughed, we cried, we revised, we persevered. We loved, had patience, had grace, but more importantly we honored and supported each other. In moments where self-support is not enough, it's okay to rely on others. As I write this, we still haven't met in person. I have this dream where we meet onstage for the first time with an audience to tell our story.

There is great perspective in asking for help, providing help, and in helping yourself. Various moments call for one of these; some moments cry for all of them. Help leads and guides you in new directions. It's those eagle eyes and different perspective that offer a different take on the situation.

When you think you need so much help with this or that, consider if you really do. Separate what moments call for asking for help from others and which ones call for the personal accountability to kick into high gear and really go all in and support yourself. You can cry, you can kick, you can scream, and sometimes when things aren't going to change for the better, you go back to that moment of choice and decide and go through the steps of change once again.

With support may come feedback. Our new selves may need to reach out for feedback. We may give ourselves permission to ask those with whom we interact and take positive view of feedback and redefine if necessary. We may or may not incorporate this feedback based on how it makes us feel to the core.

I really love these next two stories about support. Both concern the reach within for internal support, but also needed external support for survival. Both people are also tremendous givers of their time and energy, so being temporarily unable to serve others and having to ask for help has been a source of frustration for them. Both operate at impact levels of mastery and are examples of having to relearn, adjust to new circumstances, and use all points of change and all courage within to survive.

## Stories from the Heart
### Lisa Sedgwick Minakowski—Surviving and Thriving

After spending twenty wonderful years raising my two amazing children, I pursued my passion of acting and modeling. In fact, at any given moment you may find me on billboards, QVC, TV commercials, pharmaceutical campaigns, social media outlets, and fashion runways, as well as in feature films, clothing catalogs, and medical journals. With each booking, not only did my confidence grow, but so did my network of truly talented professionals. I take great pride in my career and support of the Multiple Myeloma Foundation, Breast Cancer Awareness, Myriad Genetics, Suicide Awareness, and Women in Engineering. I am also a proud original member of the Actors' Think Tank.

Because of my family medical history of breast and pancreatic cancer, in 2018 my gynecologist suggested genetic testing. A scientific link had been identified between these two cancers. My doctor offered a simple blood test (Myriad Genetic

Test) taken in the office. The results revealed I carry the ATM gene mutation, which increased my chance for breast and pancreatic cancer two to four times more than the average woman. Armed with knowledge in early 2019, I received genetic counseling and was issued my first MRI breast scan along with my yearly mammogram. Since the age of twenty-five, all previous mammograms had been normal. August 2019 was no different. A clear, beautiful, normal mammogram was taken.

September 11, 2019, however proved to be dually devastating. As I remembered those lost in the 2001 terrorist attacks on America, I received news that the MRI found five masses (one large and four smaller) in my right breast. After immediate consultation with the top breast cancer surgeon and plastic surgeon at the hospital of the University of Pennsylvania on September 30, 2019, I had a double mastectomy with DIEP flap reconstruction. I awoke twenty-four hours later to news that the sentinel lymph node tested positive for cancer—the cancer had metastasized. After one week in the hospital, I was discharged and sent home with six drains. I received round-the-clock nursing care at home for the next two months. After removal of my last drain, chemotherapy began. I chose not to have a port inserted; the idea of more cutting into my skin was nauseating. The IV was now my new best friend, even though each infusion resulted in many needle sticks, heavy bruising, and scars left from the chemical burns.

I embraced each moment, believing in science and knowing I was trying my best to overcome cancer. I honestly wanted to set a standard for my children and show them my commitment to our beautiful life. I had to accept the unexpected and remain calm. However, I did not choose to ring the bell after my last treatment. The ATM gene mutation is forever a part of me, so I remain positive but am very realistic and try to continue to stay ahead of the cancer.

Next was physical therapy for lymphedema and the stretching of my abdominal skin to be able to stand upright again (I lost over an inch in height). During my physical therapy at the Rothman Institute, I was a live model. Physical therapists in training were not only able to manipulate and work on me but also ask me questions during the training. I received many accolades and thanks from those involved.

Staying the course, monthly Lupron injections to suppress my estrogen were now on the agenda for the next five years. Unfortunately, because of the COVID pandemic and hospital restrictions (my treatments were not deemed "necessary"),

I did not receive Lupron shots until June 2020. After receiving a few shots, there became a shortage of Lupron due to shipping problems in the United States. I was no longer able to get the Lupron shots. In November 2020, I was forced to have a total hysterectomy. I faced a new world of side effects. For additional insurance against breast cancer, Arimidex is now part of my daily routine for the next ten years. It is a hormone-based chemotherapy aimed at reducing my risk of breast cancer returning.

Another side effect of the COVID pandemic was the total shutdown of the acting and modeling world. In March 2020, the Actors' Think Tank was born, of which I was an original member. Once a week via Zoom, we helped one another stay creative and positive. We also helped one another create professional home studios. Our group of acting professionals has remained a constant network of support, sharing and inspiring, and our weekly Zoom meetings continue. These calls now include nationwide casting directors, acting coaches, producers, directors, writers, attorneys, and established actors, such as Kevin Bacon!

As of March 2021, I am proud to acknowledge that I am back to work as an actor and model. I have been honored with photo shoots for AnaOno (intimate apparel line for breast cancer patients/survivors) and a new breast cancer drug campaign. Also, be sure to look for me on Primo Hoagies and Tommie Copper advertising, QVC, the feature film *Trust No One* and in a new Scrooge movie *Scrooge, A Christmas Yet to Come*.

As I look back on my breast cancer journey and research, and try to learn, I strongly believe genetic testing saved my life. Prior to my diagnosis, I had no medical symptoms. My breast cancer was a medium- to fast-growing lobular type. Had I not chosen to have the Myriad genetic blood test that random day in 2018, I would not be here today to encourage others to be advocates for their own health. I remain a believer in science and continue to trust my doctors. However, my most important takeaway has been that *family history* is very important and should not be over-looked. I strongly encourage everyone to investigate their family history. In particular, anyone with a family history of breast and pancreatic cancer should get genetic screening (this includes men). Likewise, anyone with dense breast tissue should consider opting for an MRI in addition to their yearly mammogram. #lovelifeandliveit

●  ●  ●

Please take a breath and a moment between reading these stories. Pause and wish Lisa some peace and love.

## Gary Kobat—Challenges into Gifts

The doctor walked into the emergency room at the hospital, professional looking, gruff, white coat, studious, wanting to have a word with the mother and her aspiring athlete.

"Son, I'm here to tell you that your career is over. You'll need to be walking with assistance, probably a cane, or with difficulty the rest of your life."

That is *not* the most inspiring thing to tell a twenty-two-year-old, whose lifelong goal and fifteen-year singular practice was to be a professional athlete. This man walked around with his hair on fire, while having the confidence of an entire team in his every step.

The moment of truth for that young man was a moment in a life when a key decision must be made that will chart a new course. He could align with the dark, heavy, and broken energy of being another victim and struggle the rest of his life, or he could pause, listen, and believe in the energy that got him there, given to him by something bigger than himself.

Needless to say, that young man told the doctor what he thought and who he was, without diplomacy, fighting for every ounce of human potential in his voice while appreciating the doctor's opinion, but rejecting every ounce of the doctor's vision for his own future outcome. Yes, you could hear a pin drop. Jaws dropped.

You see, there are moments when life happens *for* us, not *to* us. We call them "moments of truth"—opportunities to align with what's true or with what's false.

Know that there's a huge human and life lesson in everything we experience—moments of truth for each and every one of us; moments for us to step up, into, or own who we really are and why we're really here.

Yes, we are all students—from the moment we understand and become aware of this, and for the rest of our lives.

Oh, by the way, that young man above—that was me. *Ha.* What a deciding moment in my life that was.

Key people and doctors have pointed out to me that I have run fifty-four marathons, made four Team USA teams, participated in four world championships, have run 100,000 miles, and have ridden 500,000 miles on a bike after eight years of physical therapy on that leg since that moment.

Fast-forward twenty years: on a hot day in Los Angeles, I was pacing—running alongside—an Olympian in her final six-mile training run before a key national championship, and I couldn't run any longer. Poof. Done. Had to walk, hobble, limp, actually, back to the car three miles. Excruciating pain.

Another moment of truth for that now-seasoned, aging athlete, turned coach: align with the dark, heavy, and broken energy of being another victim and struggle the rest of my life—or pause, listen, and believe in the energy that got me there, given to me by something bigger than myself.

Needless to say, we're never really done. It's hip to have a new hip now after three years of physical therapy, as I expanded my coaching practice into the art of the comeback, training deep into the bike, expanding my mind, body, spirit, and life coaching practice to a who's who in film, business, sport, and life.

Again, we can now begin to see, life happens *for* us, not *to* us, if we choose.

Challenges are life's little wake-up calls.

Fast-forward another ten years: on a cool day in Malibu, I was pacing a well-known actor on a training ride, getting him ready for his annual northern California bike event with his friends, and I fainted at a red light. Out cold. Poof. As I woke up, he asked if he should call 911. I said of course, as I could not remember anything that had happened. Days later I'm on life support for six hours as we all agreed that the malfunctioning heart valve that took my father and grandfather needed to be replaced in me with an open heart surgery procedure so I could do what I love the rest of my life here on Earth.

Yes, yet again, another moment of truth for that seasoned, aging athlete, turned coach, with a new knee, new leg, new hip: align with the dark, heavy, and broken energy of being another victim and struggle the rest of my life—or pause, listen, and believe in the energy that got me there, given to me by something bigger than myself.

Needless to say, after three years post-op physical therapy, we all agree I'm ready for my first bike race as I write this, with new and enhanced forms of my coaching practice, grateful to be alive and giving back with the art of the comeback—developing deep, radical, meaningful sessions in transformation—mentally, physically, spiritually, and emotionally.

You see, our challenges are our gifts.

They ask us to awaken and align to the truth—to our real selves, and to the fact that we are amazing human beings, no matter what is going on in our lives . . . no matter if we have new body parts, have lost, won, gained, slimmed, lost our way, lost someone, or are finally ready for aligning with the truth, the way the divine has intended.

The real story is that we are unlimited beings. The real story is that the world and the Universe are unlimited. We are right where we're intended, and we must start telling the story of our amazing lives because whatever story we tell, light or dark, vibrational energies will make sure we receive it.

And that will be the story of our life.

● ● ●

Those are incredible stories of survival and sheer will to live. I applaud their instant yes and sharing their stories to help other people. Their attitudes are incredible. What did you learn from them? Have you or has anyone around you had a difficult moment medically?

Lisa's and Gary's stories remind me of a bunch of things. Our professional best success and everything else can be derailed in a moment with a medical crisis. I've seen it firsthand with my own life. I've seen it with my dad and my parents' business. And I've seen the multiple ways that families band together in support. I've also seen people alone with medical issues crying for assistance.

Here in this moment, we all have a responsibility to one another and humanity as a whole to do whatever we can for others. Remember that not everyone is walking around or moving around in peace. Many have multiple issues playing in the background of their lives, with many common issues related to money, grief, stress, relationships, children, and health issues. Most people have something going on that you can't see, and perhaps they don't want you to know it. Many of us like to solve our crises personally.

Be kind to all you encounter, with whatever level or type of support you need or you are providing. This includes being nice to people on the phone.

As we proceed through Exercises 9 and 10, we are going to ask questions about support, accountability, and responsibility. Please be aware this is personal and may be uncomfortable. Remember, though, that the growth and change rest heavily within that discomfort, so please be truthful. Also, remember that if you don't feel comfortable writing in this book, these exercises are all provided online at besteveryou.com/changeguidebook.

## POINTS TO PONDER

**Think. Write. Talk. Action.** *(Because practice makes us our best.)*

### EXERCISE 9: Your Powerful 20

Think with me for a moment. I call this Your Powerful 20. You can call it My Powerful _____ (place your own number here).

Think and make a list of the following:

**1. Five ways you've been helpful to other people**

_____

_____

_____

_____

_____

**2. Five ways you've been helped by other people**

_____

_____

_____

_____

_____

**3. Five ways you wish you could help other people or the world**

_____

_____

_____

_____

_____

4. Five ways you will help other people or the world

_____

_____

_____

_____

_____

## EXERCISE 10: Accountability

Copy your answers from Exercise 8 and write them here for one area:

Area of focus: _____

Statement of empowerment: _____

Goal 1: _____

Goal 2: _____

1. Identify two people you know who could help you achieve your goals.

_____

_____

2. Think of two people you need to know who could help you exceed your goals.

_____

_____

3. Think of two people who need to know you as you achieve your goals or who will help you move to the mastery level, should you desire that.

_____

_____

4. What are a few of your additional goals?

_____

_____

5. How are you going to help yourself with your goals?

_____

6. What do you need help with?

_____

7. Has anyone in your life helped you achieve your goals? Have you helped others achieve theirs?

_____

8. How do you support yourself?

_____

9. Who are the five people closest to you? Of those people, who are the two closest to you?

_____

_____

_____

_____

_____

10. Are those two people closest to you helping you achieve your goals? If so, how?

_____

_____

Write an accountability statement: a promise to yourself. Hold yourself accountable to achieve one goal for thirty days.

_____

_____

# CHAPTER 6
# IMPLEMENT

*In our sixth point, we improve and implement. We step back and look at what we have become, accept, and continue to look at ourselves honestly. We continue to refine, always staying true to becoming our Best Ever You. At this point of change, we use and continue with feedback, tools, and so forth to continue our growth and discovery.*

You are the producer and director of your own life, too, and how lucky for you: the star of the show. Congratulations!

That's easy, right? Change is as easy as 1, 2, 3.

Well, when I took a sampling of my community and told them I was writing a book about change, it was like mice scurrying to avoid me. I understand much more clearly how to get on the rides at amusement parks ahead of everyone else. Just mention the word "change," and people will run for the hills.

You're right. Implementing change can be a mental chess move. Once you've studied the board and weighed each option, it's your last and best option, and one made through careful analysis and honesty.

I just said another word that trips people up: "chess." Oh, that is so hard to play. I don't get it. So my new bumper stickers will read, "Hey, let's make some changes" and "Hey, let's play chess"—and I'll never be in traffic again.

When you implement change in that same manner, you've designed the most optimal conditions for a stronger, better, and more refined life. So the sixth point of change is to *implement*. This is a moment when we stop wishing for it and start working for it and have some fun doing the work! I promise. I promise you this won't be bad. I've got you, and you have you.

We've assessed, we've made choices, we've discovered, we've grown. We've really thought about what has happened or what we want to do to a large extent. Now it is time to take action. You will have the opportunity to step back and look at what you have become, to accept, and to continue to look at yourself honestly. We continue to refine as we commit to staying true to becoming our Best Ever You. That's all fun language for action, and we're going to take some amazing action.

It is here as we take action and really start that we succeed or we don't follow through. With those areas we may make adjustments, of course, but as I've used these points of change, usually I see one or the other. Then as the lack of follow-through happens, there is usually a scrambling to adjust in some way, followed by giving up—unless you have the right tools with you.

Here are some notes I've gathered along the way to pass along as my best implementation success tips:

- Be resolved. Be committed and be 100 percent in.
- Be consistent and disciplined.
- See through ambiguity. Be okay with not knowing how it will turn out.
- Make adjustments.
- Do the extra everything to exceed even your own expectations.

- When other people have stopped, it is your cue to work harder. Do the extra work.
- Be resilient.
- Review your goals daily or more if you need to.
- Get creative and have fun.
- Tune out the noise, gain more momentum.

This chapter makes me personally think of everything I have tried to do in my life—where I have succeeded, where I have failed, and what I keep trying no matter the outcome because I love to do it.

**What do you love to do?**

**What do you want to do?**

**When you get up in the morning, what motivates you?**

**What are you thinking about?**

Fostering positive momentum can be very useful when implementing change. Best Ever You Network member E. J. Yerzak, who is now a published author, asked himself these questions and more as he implemented a series of changes to be where he is now.

> I've always had a love-hate relationship with change. I grew up as the older of two brothers in my family, and from a very young age I developed an interest in a few things that would become my comfort zones—reading books, drawing comics, and painting. There's a trend here, of course. These are all solitary activities.
>
> Sure, I enjoyed playing sports, too, just as much as any young boy. My sports of choice were baseball and basketball. Yet even for these team sports, I really enjoyed the solitary time I would spend practicing. I would create entire basketball brackets and play against myself in the driveway to determine who would advance, simply by alternating who had possession whenever I would miss a shot. Baseball wasn't much different. My daily practice consisted of throwing a tennis ball against the chimney on our house for hours at a time.

It was no surprise that I found solace in solitary activities. I was extremely shy growing up, and as much as my parents tried to get me to come out of my so-called shell, I just couldn't do it. I had a lot going for me, it seemed. Good grades. Friendly. But as hard as I tried, I had trouble talking to people I didn't know that well. I couldn't look coaches in the eye, preferring instead to stare down at my shoes. I was out of my element, out of my comfort zone, and I felt like I didn't belong on the bench alongside my teammates. I was an average player, but my lack of confidence proved to be my largest obstacle.

I knew I needed to change and wanted to change. But I felt immobilized. I didn't know how to change. And then, one day, it just started to click for me. I began to embrace my uniqueness, slowly at first, and then in larger and larger increments as I observed that my friends didn't view me any differently as I grew more comfortable in my own skin.

One day on a whim in high school, I grabbed my dad's VHS camcorder and recorded a skit about a cross-country runner who kept trying to avoid practice by finding great hiding places. I was the runner who kept hiding. My classmates seemed to love the ridiculous videos (and this was well before the Internet was accessible to a high school student and before YouTube and TikTok existed). One video quickly led to more, and I found myself having fun with it all.

Maybe it was a little bit of teenage cockiness mixed with senioritis that kick-started my awareness. I started to embrace my individuality and began feeling more confident in choosing to do things because I wanted to do them, not because I felt that I had to do them. Looking back, in three pivotal instances I took this message to heart, finding the courage deep within to put myself out there.

First, during senior year of high school, I wasn't good enough to make the varsity basketball team and probably barely made the J.V. team. However, my school also fielded a first-year squad. I had the privilege of being a senior while my younger brother was one of the freshmen on this team, and I branched out of my comfort zone to do something unexpected. I asked the J.V. coach if I could be transferred down to the first-year team. "Why would you want to do that?" was an easy question to answer. I wanted to play basketball on a team with my brother. It would be the only opportunity I would ever have to play on the same high school basketball team as my brother. I seized the moment.

Two years later at Colgate University, the change in me progressed even more. Those cheesy VHS video clips I used to make had remained a burning passion for me, and I realized that I wanted to make an actual movie. What better time than while I had access to the cameras and editing software at our college TV station? The AV club on campus was a small group, and borrowing the equipment for projects was actually encouraged. Fortunately, my roommate at the time was excited about the idea as well, and over the course of our winter break we managed to pen a 150-page screenplay. The response on campus to the casting call notices was wonderful, and over the course of nine months, I proceeded to film about ten hours of video and edit it down to a nearly two-hour movie. I presented it to a standing-room-only crowd in the largest auditorium on campus, and the college newspaper wrote a feature story that made the front page.

Fast-forward to 2020, and my change came full circle. I wrote and published my first novel, *Access Point*, by far one of the scariest things I have done. I pledged to donate the first-year proceeds from my book to the Alzheimer's Association and to a local animal rescue charity.

Nowadays, I travel across the country for work as a cybersecurity expert, and I have spoken at conferences halfway around the world. I volunteer as a Little League coach and take extra time to instill confidence in the kids on my team, so hopefully they can recognize their own unique abilities far sooner than I did. My friends today who knew me growing up can't believe that the same shy kid they used to know is now speaking onstage in front of audiences, coaching a team, and putting a movie and a book out in the wild.

For me, change wasn't instantaneous like in the movies. My transformation was far more gradual. But if I could change one more thing, I'd go back in time. And I would leave a note to my younger self: "What are you waiting for?"

Professionally, people generally hang out with me at some point to improve aspects of their lives. (Although I secretly know it is for chocolate chip cookies!) Seriously, I've helped a lot of people lose a lot of weight as part of my coaching practice. "Eat less, move more, stay consistent" is my theory—and my own practice when I need to shed pounds. However, minds play more games with that simple action than any of us would ever care to probably consider. The health industry would not be such a moneymaker if that weren't the case. Generally, I help my clients implement a series of small changes for their best success.

## SUCCESS TIP #24: Make a Series of Small Changes That Will Compound

Often it starts with one small change that has a ripple effect, as I described in my first book, *PERCOLATE: Let Your Best Self Filter Through*.

One of the best ways to make a change is to implement small daily changes and hold them for thirty days. Here is a three-month plan that will work for most changes you want to make.

**Month 1: Make a change for thirty days.**

**Month 2: Keep going with Month 1's change, add a second change, and make that one for thirty days.**

**Month 3: Keep going with Month 1's change and Month 2's change. Add a third change for thirty days.**

By the end of ninety days, you have made three small changes that yield long-lasting results.

Here is an example based on one of my clients. Weighing 287 pounds,

Susan admitted she had lost track of her value system. Susan finally broke through the numbness of being stuck by admitting that fast food was her go-to stress reliever, and that after a busy or difficult day, the ease and comfort of the greasy, unhealthy food de-escalated her feelings of failure, disappointment, and dejection. It was an easier state to be in than one that would require honestly examining herself and maintaining these habits that were destroying any shred of contentment and pride.

To get to those moments required truth and to be in touch with how Susan was really feeling. She knew her goal and how she dreamed of being and feeling, but she couldn't understand why, if she could see *that*, she couldn't string together consistent days of change to produce the results she was seeking.

Her goal was to remove at least 100 pounds, and she had no idea where to begin. From the get-go, I felt like solid support for Susan. I was her secret best friend, rooting for her success, because I knew she could do it in what I was hearing from her. She just needed to make a few small changes to produce the results.

When I met with Susan, she felt like her actual behavior was so far down a path of being nearly the opposite of what she valued: well-being. Discovering Susan was on a high-speed train fueled by a sugar addiction and medication, I saw how she felt out of line with her values and goals. When I met Susan, she claimed to value her health and well-being, obsessing over those alleged values, yet crying and bingeing on fast food each day. Susan was used to checking in at New Year's for resolutions that had failed time and time again.

Susan released those 100 pounds over the course of a year, by aligning her heart, truths, and energy. Most of the work we did together was in the realm of her value system and thinking from her heart, instead of her brain. We also achieved success by making one small change at a time and then holding it for a period before introducing another. In the first few months, we made no changes to what Susan was eating; instead we changed what she was drinking and then added to what she was already eating, as you will see below. Soon, Susan had multiple changes in the works. We did our assessments and so forth, and here were some of the actions Susan took over the year. Please notice how the small actions compound.

**Month 1: Susan drank only water (a proper amount of water for her) and decaf green tea. The first ten days involved a caffeine detox and withdrawal.**

**Month 2: Susan continued drinking only water and decaf green tea. Next she added one cup of fresh or steamed vegetables to her lunch each day.**

**Month 3: Susan continued drinking only water and decaf green tea and adding one cup of vegetables to her food each day. Next, she added twenty minutes of walking each day, rain or shine.**

**Month 4: She continued all the changes from Month 3 (water, veggies, walking) and decreased the size of her food portions by half.**

**Month 5: Everything in Month 4, and Susan began drinking green smoothies for breakfast each day.**

**Month 6: Added another 20 minutes of exercise to everything in Month 5.**

**Month 7: Susan bought so many new clothes and held all her changes together for one month without changing anything. Susan was successful in staying consistent.**

**Month 8: Susan keep all changes from Months 6 and 7 and removed dairy from her diet.**

**Month 9: Susan booked a cruise and kept all changes going.**

**Month 10: Susan joined a gym and kept all changes going.**

**Month 11: Susan walked a half marathon.**

**Month 12: Susan weighed in 100 pounds lighter and kept all changes going.**

I suggested to implement a moment-to-moment practice. Susan had to wait a full five to ten minutes before she ate anything. It took some adjustment. She also discovered the truth and realized the truth. She had been going through a drive-through as many as three to six times a day. She described herself as being on autopilot in a way, doing things without thinking. We discovered this habit with an honest food log. This had what I consider bonus ripple effects because as soon as Susan stopped going through the drive-through, she discovered she had more money as well. At first, Susan felt like she had a bit of the fun disturbed from her life. As we added things back in, she made healthier food choices but kept the joy of doing something she liked to do: hitting a drive-through. You'll hear me say that awareness might create a more boring feeling sometimes, but being in line with your values aids in controlling addictions or other compulsive behaviors that have caused you to drift from your real values. You might be a person who needs to create this pause to realign with your values, as Susan did.

Susan went on her cruise 100 pounds lighter, healthier than ever, and off four medications, with the cooperation of her physician. One other medication dosage was lowered also, due to her lower weight.

Susan learned that her value system guides her heart. The trouble is that so much thinking and life were getting in the way. Susan discovered that her values required action and follow-up.

One big reason Susan was successful is that she used action and implemented her actions in line with her truth and vision and was 100 percent committed. She stopped thinking about how hard it was going to be; in fact, Susan will tell you it was fun as we framed it as a lifetime cruise adventure and created a vision statement for Susan in which she could see herself as she wanted to be and took actions that were in alignment with Susan as she lost more and more weight. Susan was realistic. She made multiple small changes that yielded huge results. Susan's support team of her husband and children also didn't sabotage her efforts, but rather they understood the yearlong plan and what it was going to take. In fact, midway through, her husband joined in and lost twenty-five pounds as well. Susan made an impression and had an impact on her husband while learning herself. Fantastic!

Let's hear from Dave Strauss and Brian Hilliard, who have implemented change in their lives.

## Stories from the Heart
### Dave Strauss—Seeking Joy

We are introduced to this world inherently seeking joy. We naturally know how to find that which bring us happiness. We also know how to avoid those things that bring us displeasure, fear, or even pain. Yet as we grow older, we can forget how to actively seek joy. We allow ourselves to become conditioned to the acceptance of displeasure. We misplace our passions, become lost in the experiences of life, and forget to implement change.

I'll share some of my experiences with you. In some, I am clearly an active participant, choosing my best path. In others, I became a passive participant. I simply allowed things to happen and fell into whatever came my way. Through this journey, I realized I needed to take control, implement change, and follow what brings me joy to be my best.

I can clearly recall being anxious as a child. It has always been a part of me. I was extremely shy as a youngster, the type of child you see hug closely to their mother's leg in an attempt to slow the introduction to new people. I understand now I also had some level of obsessive-compulsive disorder (OCD). For example, my dresser was always immaculately organized with everything in its assigned place. If something lost its place, I would quickly restore it to the assigned spot to reestablish the natural order. I recognize this today mainly in what I refer to as my skill of dishwasher organization. If this were an Olympic sport, I would no doubt be a gold medal winner. Or at a minimum, I should star in an advertisement for KitchenAid!

Yet this anxious side of me lived in harmony with another part of my personality, which was a very natural calmness. I was always taking things as they came. I actively sought fun and any type of adventure. Throughout my youth and into early adulthood, meeting people and making friends came naturally. I was also the person who tried to be the glue. My goal was always to bring friends and disparate groups together. And I am fortunate to this day to have a melting pot of friendships and experiences. This natural ease and balance between a bit of anxiety and my chillaxed side defined me through early adulthood.

At the age of nineteen, my older brother wanted to move to Florida. With my best friend, the three of us packed up a car and off we went to Florida. After a month in a hotel, when Florida didn't quite work out, we moved home to regroup. A month or so later, we decided to give Maryland a try. And one more time, the three of us packed up and moved to Baltimore, Maryland. We landed comfortably in Baltimore, I believe naturally so, as this was my mother's hometown, and most of the maternal side of my family still lived there. I brought with me the willingness to try just about anything, to speak to just about anyone, and to easily build relationships.

Meeting people and enjoying experiences marked this time of my life. I remember a trip to Las Vegas and arranging for tickets to see Redd Foxx. After the show, I was bold enough to sneak backstage. I somehow was not noticed by security and removed as I might have expected. I ended up being able to meet Redd Foxx, and I have a picture of us together that I still treasure to this day.

Then there was the day I saw a former American League Rookie of the Year waiting uncomfortably by the entrance to the retailer where I was working at the time. We grew up in the same region of Indiana, and I decided I would strike up a conversation. I quickly understood that his discomfort related to the taxi he was waiting for running late. Having just been traded to the Baltimore Orioles, he did not want to be late on his first game day. What to do, what to do? Well, of course, we jumped into my 1979 Buick LeSabre. I drove him to Memorial Stadium, the home of the Orioles. We talked and laughed the entire drive. I ended up with two tickets to that night's game for the gesture.

But looking back now, I know I let myself lose that person: the person who was excited to move to a new city, the person who was willing to jump into a fun situation and see what might come. In life, we sometimes allow ourselves to be led to varying degrees of what I describe as falling asleep at the wheel. We let ourselves drift from who we are at our core. And we can end up forgetting to avoid the displeasure and to search out joy.

I gradually became a master on the hamster wheel of average American adult life. I left my job as a teacher, going back to work in the corporate world. Why? Well, isn't that what we do to provide for our families? I eventually married a person who was wrong for me. I would wake up, brush my teeth, shower, and then go off to work like clockwork each weekday, my OCD probably working to my advantage, finding some level of comfort in the unhappiness of the minutiae. And of course, this portion of life wouldn't be complete without a bad diet, sedentary lifestyle, and series of questionable career decisions.

With each passing day this continued on some level for almost fifteen years—a blur from my midtwenties to almost forty. My five-foot-eight, 198-pound self, daily sufferer of heartburn, had little to no idea what happened. Yet fortunately one day I saw through this haze. Enjoying a fast-food value meal in my cubicle, it hit me that age forty was on the horizon. I had a moment when I saw through to the 130-pound happy, healthy version of myself. I knew as the clock ticked toward forty, time was of the essence. I was careening toward life-altering health issues. I also knew once I crossed the threshold past forty, it would just become more difficult to make a change.

In that moment, at my desk, I finally began the process of saying enough. I pulled out the calendar and counted the number of days until birthday number forty. I dedicated myself to a goal of forty workouts in the forty days before my fortieth birthday. I hit the gym five days a week for forty to forty-five minutes on the elliptical machine. I began cutting out the bad stuff. I eliminated what I call "the whites" from my diet. No more white sugar, white flour, or table salt. And the journey back to me began.

My unhappy marriage happily ended. I met the love of my life. My family of two became a family of five as my daughter and I welcomed my new wife and her sons to our family. And the new marriage and bigger family became six as we welcomed a baby girl one year later. Things were going well, better than in years. I was following a process to a better me. Change was gaining momentum, but I met the inevitable plateau.

I was eating better, but was I eating well? I was working out, but was I really challenging myself? At that point, working with my wife, we switched to a high-protein, low- to no-carb approach to nutrition. Where before I worked out alone, I found the courage to step into group exercise classes. I was at the gym at 5:30 in the morning five to six days a week for a mix of strength and cardio training. I would also attend the occasional yoga class. Through this journey, I have been able to lose fifty pounds, weight that will never return. Long-ago diagnoses of sleep apnea and acid reflux were now a thing of the past.

The uphill momentum of change had shifted downhill. There was no turning back now, but there was still this calling. I knew there was another level of happiness still eluding me. I was working on the physical me, yet I was still on the hamster wheel of waking up and working each day, each week, for the weekend. I was wound tight and full of worry about any shoe that might drop next. I realized I was still neglecting the emotional and spiritual sides of me.

The loss of my dad gave me a hidden blessing. I was fortunate to be with him and work from his hospice room for his last two weeks of life. In the time afterward, as I processed the loss of my father, it was literally one of those moments in the shower. Standing quietly, water pouring over my head, I had an epiphany. I believe it was a message from Dad. My dad was a worrier, and that trait had gradually worsened as he aged. Yet I knew in that moment, he didn't want me to spend one more moment wasted in worry. And it was time to get off the hamster wheel and truly search out happiness.

With the loss of my father as the impetus, I was able to lean into the emotional and spiritual phase of my growth. And I knew this couldn't be done alone. I found a life coach, an amazing person who helped me visualize this journey back to myself. She helped me recognize that our children are our greatest teachers. She also helped me see the value in each present moment, a practice of gratitude, and the importance of chasing our passions. I was introduced to meditation. Stepping aside from strength training, I made yoga my workout of choice.

At this time, I also felt a calling to begin writing. Writing is something I have always wanted to do, but I had only done some personal journaling when I was younger. My wife and I started a website, and I began blogging. I met Elizabeth and joined the Best Ever You Network. The community Elizabeth has built is incredibly supportive and uplifting. I began sharing blogs to besteveryou.com, and the momentum of happiness was amazing. It was such an adrenaline rush to post a new blog to the site and share it through social media.

I believe when you are chasing your passions, amazing things begin to happen for you. Elizabeth introduced me to a publisher, encouraging me to pitch ideas I had for children's books. And I can proudly say that I am now a published children's book author of the Rugby Bugby series and *A Turkey Named Spaghetti*. And isn't it funny how things come full circle? Recently I came across some old documents and journals. As I leafed through them, I found ideas about children's books I had hoped to write someday. Not coincidentally, those notes, which I hadn't seen for twenty years, align with the themes of the books I am writing today. And I realized, I am back. I am myself again. But that doesn't mean the work is done. It means the juicy part is just beginning.

Fourteen years into my path of change, I enjoy helping others find their passions, too. The first step can feel like the biggest and scariest. But one step is all it takes. Be honest with where you are and where you want to go. A simple workout schedule and subtle changes in how we eat can be a great start. Set interim goals and celebrate every step of the way. Small wins lead to big momentum, and the thirst for change and continuous improvement grow. My biggest piece of advice may be this: Don't be afraid to ask for help. I encourage you to seek a coach. Find an expert to help support you in whatever area(s) of growth are important to you. And leverage communities like the Best Ever You Network. The content, community, and support you will find are amazing.

Knowing that I needed to make a physical change is when this began. I now place just as much importance on my emotional health. I meditate and practice gratitude daily. I also like to find time for reading and writing each day. I believe to my core that the decrease in my worry and increase in connection to my true self has improved as a result of a few simple practices. I know that with meditation, gratitude, and focusing on joy each day, the work of being the best version of me continues.

### Brian Hilliard—Go-Getter

Truth be told, I was always considered a go-getter.

Good grades in high school, played on the football team, got accepted to Duke University, got hired by GE Capital and was accepted in their prestigious Management Development Program, finished that two-year program three months early (never been done before) to accept a full-time position in Chicago as a team developer, still for GE, and got recruited to another corporation where I worked for three years in Atlanta.

So it didn't come as a surprise when I decided to start my own business back in 2001.

That's what go-getters did, right?

And if we're really being honest, I actually liked that reputation.

I was the guy people came to when they wanted to get things done. And most of the time I actually did make it happen.

But here's when I knew there was a problem.

On my first week out on my own, I realized that I couldn't work after lunch.

You see, I was soooo amped up and such a go-getter that my stomach got worked up to the point where I literally was not able to do any work after I ate. My doctor told me it was a function of all the stress I had in corporate (preulcer conditions at age twenty-six and twenty-eight), and at twenty-nine, I was still dealing with the effects.

*No problem!* I thought.

I started getting up super early (like 4:30 AM) and made it a point to do eight hours of work *before* my regular 1 PM lunch time. That way I could still get stuff done, eat lunch, then I wound up reading a business book for the next couple of hours and called it a day. (That turned out to be a blessing in disguise, because reading didn't bother my stomach at all, which allowed me to build up a really good base of knowledge that I still use today as a coach.)

*Problem solved!* I thought.

Well, it turned out that the outside symptoms of the problem had been solved, but as far as the actual problem itself—there was still some meat left on *that* bone.

But at the time, I didn't realize it—until a few months later I got really sick. Like, can't get off the couch sick. Like, can't watch television or read a book because I'm that dizzy sick. And I was like that for a week.

Now in hindsight, I should have realized that this was my body's way of telling me to slow down, smell the roses. You don't have to be *such* a go-getter *all* the time.

But I didn't listen. After I got better, I jumped right in again! And I got sick (again), a few months later. Exact same symptoms, exact same time-out on the couch: one week.

Unfortunately, once again, I missed the exact same message my body was trying to tell me.

After I got better, I jumped right back into the business (again), with full force!

And by now you probably know what happened, of course: I got sick . . . again! This time—while lying on the couch, not being able to read or watch TV or do much of anything—I finally got the message.

"Brian!" my body said. "You really need to slow down a bit."

"Slow down! I can't do that," I replied. "I've got a business to run."

"Yes, I totally understand, but you can't keep running your business at this pace, otherwise we [you] are going to completely break down physically. We [you] simply can't keep up this breakneck pace anymore."

And that's when I finally got it.

At age thirty-two I realized that I had to come up with a different way of doing things, otherwise my body was going to literally stop working.

And obviously I didn't want *that* to happen, but I also didn't want to be considered a sloth, laggard, or whatever word one uses to characterize the opposite of a go-getter.

So after thinking about it, talking to some folks, and then thinking about it some more, I finally realized a few truths.

*Truth #1: Who you are is* not *what you do.*

In other words, I was looking at my personal and professional accomplishments as a little bit of a proxy for how I wanted to be perceived. And it wasn't like I was over the top in this area, but I was a little closer to making this error in thinking than perhaps I initially realized.

I had to come to terms with the fact that who I am had nothing to do with what I did.

Who I am was measured by how I showed up and how people felt while being around me. Who I am was picking someone up at the airport or helping a friend move. Who I am was taking time to listen, even when I'm in a hurry. Who I am is being the type of person whom people liked being around.

That had nothing to do with what I did.

And like I said before, even though I didn't consider myself to be out of control in this area, I did realize that it could be something where I could use a little work.

I considered it a good start.

*Truth #2: I didn't have to be soooo serious and go-getterly* all *the time. In other words, I had to learn to relax.*

This one took me a lot longer to truly embrace, but I remember playing golf with some clients one time in Houston and I realized, *You know . . . if I could approach my life like I did a round of golf, I think I would be a lot better off.*

And what I meant by that is when I play golf, I'm usually focused *and* relaxed at the same time.

Obviously, I'm focused when figuring out the type of shot to hit, which club to use, and standing over my ball. But after that, I'm totally relaxed in the golf cart, driving to the green or talking to my playing partners.

I realized that off the course I was really good at the focused part but not so much on the relaxing part.

After thinking about it some more, it turns out that part of the problem was I didn't have a real hobby, something outside work that held my interest and I looked forward to doing. I started developing some.

I got more intentional in reading fiction books (turns out the *Star Wars* franchise has a *lot* of books that are very good—I started with *Death Star*, where they were actually building it from scratch), watching movies (Netflix and physically in the theaters), and even taking naps on the weekends.

I noticed a dramatic uptick in my relaxation quotient and felt a lot more refreshed heading into the workweek. Who knew?

*Truth #3: I had to learn to simplify.*

I can't emphasize this enough. I used to have a tendency to overcomplicate things and get in my own way a lot. I didn't know that about myself until some fourteen years later, but that was totally me. So I learned to simplify in every aspect of my life.

First, I had to learn how to let things go. I didn't need to let so many things bother me on such a consistent basis. Second, I toned down the level of judgment and criticality I directed toward others. I didn't realize it until *much* later, but by giving myself and others some room for error, whatever they or I did simply didn't bother me as much. I call that giving people space and grace.

Third, I cleaned up my physical work and living environment. I was living in an apartment at the time, so it wasn't like there was too much to do, but I got things straightened up. I folded laundry and put away dishes in a timely fashion. My desk— well, I'm still working on that one, but you get the idea. I made it a point to really have my physical area—the places that I see every day—just look cleaner and more inviting.

And like I said before, I can't overemphasize this enough. When your physical area is fresh and tidy, your mind finds it easier to relax. And when your mind finds it easier to relax, your body doesn't have a problem following. And when your body follows, then your work actually gets better throughout the entire week.

And as a spiritual person, I believe that there's a life purpose for all of us. And it's not our job to figure it out, just to get out of our own way long enough so we can get to wherever we need to go.

When I look back at the events that unfolded in my life and how they allowed me to be the person, speaker, business owner, and coach that I am today, I can honestly say that I wouldn't have it any other way.

Because those changes allowed me to become the person who I am today, and I am now a master of time management and mind-set in my life, and I champion these qualities daily.

●  ●  ●

Dave Strauss and Brian Hilliard's stories remind us to have faith in ourselves as we pivot or do a full-course correction. In doing so, it might feel like that terribly turbulent flight you're stuck on and you are thinking, *I need a parachute—NOW!* and then your mind takes you to how much hell that would be, too. So you feel stuck, but you know the odds are that the plane will go through the turbulence and you'll land. As you walk off the plane you think, *Okay, I survived that. I can do just about anything.*

Personally, many years ago now, I got a divorce and a few days later boarded one of the more turbulent flights I've ever experienced. I'll never forget that flight. I felt like I was being punished for needing out of a situation. It was one of the most important flights I've ever taken because as we were bouncing around all over various altitudes and people were throwing up and praying, I scribbled in my journal, "If I live through this, what am I going to do with my life?" And while I haven't ever made that list public, you're currently reading one of my goals on it.

I gathered my closest friends, family, and advisors; described my plan; and made the change, even though I was aware it may be met with concern or doubt from others. Implementation can cause an influx of contrary opinions, but (here's where that heart alignment stuff is *good*) when you've committed to the work and self-redesign, let the lessons learned guide your next move. Most importantly, any change must have self-reflection at the core.

As we move to Exercises 11 and 12, we are going to set goals and take action with a plan called MAP: Motivation, Action, Plan. Please be aware this is personal and may be uncomfortable. The growth and change rest heavily within that discomfort, so once again please be truthful and honest with yourself and anyone helping you.

## POINTS TO PONDER

**Think. Write. Talk. Action.** *(Because practice makes us our best.)*

### EXERCISE 11: Who, What, Where, Why, When, and How— MAP Out Your Plan

Copy your information for one area from Exercise 8 or 10:

**Area of focus:** _____

**Statement of empowerment:** _____

Goal 1: _____

Goal 2: _____

### MAP SYSTEM (Motivation, Action, Plan)

**Specific change:** _____

**Motivation** (What is your why? What is motivating you?):

_____

_____

_____

## ACTION (Identify two very specific actions you are going to take, one for each goal):

_____

_____

_____

**Plan** (What's your time frame? Daily? Weekly? Monthly?):

_____

_____

_____

## EXERCISE 12: Let's Go All In with Accountability

Pick a date and let's do it.

**Write down your starting date:** _____

**What are you going to do?**

Action 1: _____

Action 2: _____

## ACCOUNTABILITY

**Are you holding yourself accountable?**

_____

_____

_____

**Are you working with someone to hold yourself accountable?**

_____

_____

_____

**How are you holding yourself accountable?**

_____

_____

_____

_____

### READY-SET-GO: What daily action or actions do you do to stay on track with your goal?

_____

_____

_____

## Let's Begin Our Best Ever You Daily

As we think, write, and talk in our Points to Ponder exercises, here are seven sets of questions you can ask yourself. I've structured them so that you have a conversation with yourself day by day, with one group of questions for each day of the week. I personally prefer the one-topic-per-day approach, which I then repeat each week throughout the entire year. However, I do love to ask myself a few of these questions daily, such as: How am I feeling? Is there something in my life, perhaps underlying, that is bringing me stress or joy? What's really going on? How am I going to carry and conduct myself today? This can be a great tone setter, especially during difficult moments.

## MONDAY

How am I feeling? Is anything in my life bringing me stress or joy? What am I brewing?

_____

_____

_____

## TUESDAY

How am I going to conduct myself today? What is my behavior going to be like? Is the day going to carry me, or am I going to carry the day?

_____

_____

_____

## WEDNESDAY

What is my why? Do I have a strong sense of self and purpose?

_____

_____

_____

## THURSDAY

Where am I in life right now? Is there something I'd like to change?

_____

_____

_____

## FRIDAY

What is my self-talk like? Am I kind to myself?

_____

_____

_____

## SATURDAY

Who are the people with whom I spend the most time? How is their behavior compared to mine?

_____

_____

_____

## SUNDAY

How do I spend my time? For a week, I'll look at twenty-four-hour periods and list how I spend each day. Is there a pattern? What are my intentions? What actions have I taken to change my intention into action?

_____

_____

_____

# CHAPTER 7
# ACCEPT

*In this point, we examine our attitude and develop a process of what matters most. We focus on the art of realizing that each moment matters and how to be in decision in each moment, all while bringing our unique talents and gifts and realizing our inner light. This is a moment of allowing and accepting the truth deep within, to live authentically and move forward.*

**When your life feels like an** out-of-control three-ring circus, remember: you are the ringmaster.

## SUCCESS TIP #25: Take Responsibility for Every Aspect of Yourself

You are the chief operating officer, chief creative officer, chief visionary officer, chief compliance officer, and whatever kind of C-suite title you want to hold. The power in you and in this book continues to be in your hands and on these pages and in their exercises.

In this chapter we fine-tune and really align with our heart and truths. Our energy is coming around with us. You are going to focus on shifting your attitude to become the best personal strategic thinker you can be. There is healing in acceptance. You may need to let go or make space. You may need to own your mistakes, push through fear, embrace joy, and celebrate the wins. Acceptance has so many aspects, including tolerance, patience, and time. So in this point of change we continue to develop a way to align our energy to what matters most. In acceptance, we align to the art of realizing that each moment matters and we can decide in each moment how to be—all the while bringing our own unique talents and gifts and realizing our inner light.

Acceptance can be really easy, as in, "We have a deal. I accept." It can also be really confusing, as in, "I accept my current situation and I'd like to create my future, as I still crave changes." Acceptance doesn't mean that now is the way things have to be forever. Acceptance doesn't mean you can have your beautiful present and not add more to it. Accept the truth.

The practice of acceptance is having or making peace with what you want to change or what has changed and allowing things to change if they need to going forward. Acceptance is not an endorsement for stagnation. It's more of an acknowledgment of the present moment and the potential future and to help you not be stuck in the past. Put another way, you give yourself permission to change, with a layer of being peaceful about it, as needed. Sometimes healing is needed first in order to accept.

The work of healing requires trust, patience, and time. It involves ditching the life-isn't-fair, woe-is-me type of head noise where we resist reality, or we try to manifest with no action steps. Rather, this is thanking life for everything—the good and the bad—and training or retraining our brain to see things positively and perhaps even nudging ourselves forward through fear.

We can't have a conversation about acceptance without also understanding it is also okay to not accept. In fact, when we don't accept, sometimes our lives lead us in a new direction—for example, "I don't accept your job," or "No" to a marriage proposal.

## SUCCESS TIP #26: The Phrase "I Don't Accept" Can Be the Precipice for Change

There's a nonacceptance within the acceptance. For example, one of my clients no longer wanted to have a garage filled with clutter, so they stopped accepting that it was okay to be this way, said thank-you for the moments, acknowledged their great work in acquiring so much clutter, and then acknowledged and accepted the changes that needed to be made. Together, their family cleaned out the garage.

Within acceptance is trusting yourself, owning your mistakes and your part. Acceptance is a process. You may want it to be a solid mass, but acceptance can sway and falter. It may represent a moment, event, or result that was undesirable, painful, or even catastrophic. Acceptance doesn't mean decoding your memory to wipe it out, but rather finding a new slot for it, one that is smaller or narrower, to let peace filter through.

I wasn't going to go about losing twenty pounds by getting up each morning and screaming at myself internally for having gained twenty pounds. Honestly, I probably would have gained ten more with that line of thinking. Instead, I applied the love and acceptance and points of change I discuss within these pages to make things different. I also have a life-long medical condition: life-threatening food allergies. For quite some time when I was younger, I was unaccepting of these newfound allergies. It took a moment with my dad having a stroke and being in a rehab facility—which I talk about in my first book, *PERCOLATE*—for me to clearly understand acceptance. I was going to have this. Was I going to duke it out with myself each day or accept it and then do things like join communities that are trying to understand why people have food allergies? I've joined many groups, and I help the younger kids and adults better know how to navigate our world, which includes millions of people with life-threatening food allergies. I have healed the wounds I felt.

## SUCCESS TIP #27: Heal Your Wounds

Are you in the boxing ring with yourself in each corner?

As I was writing this book and testing it, one thing that popped up in our discussion group (my mini book club, as I like to call it) was this notion that acceptance should be the first point of change. Oh, did we have some chats about that one. As you read this, feel free to chat with me about it, too. I'm all ears and heart, and it may have to go into the category of things you aren't going to see changed. Here's why I disagree, and that's okay. I really believe in my heart of hearts and from working with people that so many people haven't really accepted the change or the circumstance, often for quite some time—and even then, some people are stuck in life, unable to accept something. They go around and around in this condition and exist with unhappiness often brewing and perhaps even festering into something worse.

I think that acceptance really is part of the process—maybe even in bits and pieces throughout—but I firmly believe that if you use my definition of acceptance during the Ten Points of Change process, it will allow you to move forward to align with your energy and highest power. The more we accept, the stronger we get; the stronger we get, the more we accept—and that's a better cycle to be in because it fosters change.

There are so many viewpoints about change. If you search the Internet for information on personal change, it seems everyone has their opinion and often that opinion is that change is scary. Well, it depends on what you allow and accept as your change viewpoint. My guess is this: If you weren't open to change or didn't want to change something, you certainly wouldn't be reading this sentence. (Give me a shout-out in social media #ChangeGuidebook if you agree! Woo-hoo—you're a change master in the making! Yes!)

Your brain may or may not feel like it is cooperating with you at all moments. I had this happen just the other day. As I shared with you, I have been losing weight. Well, my brain and mind went all Doritos on me. With my severe food allergies, when I find something I love to eat and I'm not allergic to, I have to contain myself or down goes, in this case, the whole bag of Doritos. Well, someone brought them into the house. As my eyes honed in on the big red bag, it was Doritos on the brain, change out the door, diet out the door. I was fixated on Doritos. A few wouldn't hurt, right? I'll just admit it: I ate the whole bag. Change plan destroyed. Did that moment stop my success, or do I do better the next time that telltale bag comes in the house unannounced and unhidden? If I don't stop access to my triggers—which are pizza, cookies, chocolate, and Doritos—and really root in self-love and self-worth, I could be mindlessly back to gaining those pounds I lost and back to my 2018–2019 self. I'm proud that my brain on change has left the Doritos untouched for someone else to enjoy, even while they are in plain sight. I'm stronger this time around. For me, the more times that I disregard the Doritos, the more likely I will disregard them the next time, as my brain retrains to a new way of doing things.

But let's say your brain doesn't cooperate with you and down goes the whole bag. Pick another scenario where you are going to feel off-track and perhaps fail or even become depressed about it. Our brains love that stuff, and that is really what we are overcoming and accepting: our brain training. This book is helping you to train your brain to change, to accept change, and to allow for change—and giving you the tools and resources to align your heart, your truths, and your energy. Then anything is possible. Your brain will train to whatever motivates and inspires you.

Also under acceptance falls what we absolutely can't change. I'm sorry about this one, as I have wished so hard for everyone on everything I can think of since I was a little kid. I have more prayers and thoughts and energy for people, but no matter what, I just can't seem to slow down time. You can't either. Scientists are working on it somewhere, somehow, I'm sure. Time is one thing that is charging forward on a steady beat whether you like it or not. Please accept that, because once you do, you may slow down and realize that your moments are extremely precious—and those are all moments you absolutely can't get back. Once the moment is gone, it is history. You'll hear people say to anchor in the present. I'm for a lot of that, but I also love future thinking—not to try to control the future, as we know we can't do that, but I love making plans. Just today, as a matter of fact, I was visualizing future moments with my husband.

However, one reason finding inner peace is hard is that we try to force the future, especially when we are uncomfortable with ambiguity or have anxiety about an outcome. When we have a change that we didn't want or plan for, it can throw us for such a loop that we have one of two reactions: It feels magical, serendipitous, and meant to be, or it can result in a never-ending wait for your beautiful future to land in your lap again. You wish things were the way they were before—that you could wave a wand and, voila, things are all as they should be and will never change again and you know exactly how every moment is going to turn out.

A lot of adjusting and going around and around occurs in the steps of change, with time helping us in our shifts. Ambiguity, trial and error, lack of confidence, drawing up new plans, and more are all wrapped up in this gift we call "patience." Patience really is a virtue, and many of us have to learn it and remind ourselves constantly to be patient and maybe even kind with it. Patience isn't a phase or fad.

Think of yourself as a teacher with a classroom of twenty kindergarteners. Think about the level of patience and kindness required in that daylong occupation. What if you were being snappy, rude, and mean and made every single child cry? How would that go for the kids and you? I know that is exaggerated to make the point, but it is just one small example of where patience is mandatory.

Just the other day a huge pickup truck passed me on the right and sped up to about ninety miles per hour. My husband and I both said, "What a jerk." I thought for a second and said out loud to remind us, "What if that is an emergency?" In fact, what if that is a doctor going to the hospital to perform emergency surgery? The perspective of patience can be lost in a moment of anger or frustration.

Patience goes with acceptance. You need one to get the other. Patience and acceptance are twins that function together.

There's no doubt that waiting for something could be one of the most frustrating things ever. Whether it's waiting in traffic, waiting for someone to get ready for a night out, waiting for someone to pay you, waiting in line, waiting for the weight to finally come off, and so on. Waiting can try your patience. If you take a glimpse at all these scenarios I've just listed, even if a person in front of you is taking forever or a person is delayed in sending you money, it's really about you and your ability or inability to sit peacefully with time and your patience levels.

Here are eight ways to help make patience your very best virtue.

1. *Understand patience.* Patience is the ability to wait. Patience is having the capacity to accept or tolerate delay, trouble, or suffering without getting angry or upset or impatient. I like Wikipedia's definition: "Patience (or forbearing) is the ability to endure difficult circumstances. Patience may involve perseverance in the face of delay; tolerance of provocation without responding in disrespect/ anger; or forbearance when under strain, especially when faced with longer-term difficulties. Patience is the level of endurance one can have before disrespect."

2. *Understand impatience.* Impatience comes when someone is angry, provoked, or restlessly eager. I like Webster's definitions:
   - Not willing to wait for something or someone: not patient
   - Wanting or eager to do something without waiting
   - Showing that you do not want to wait: showing a lack of patience

3. *Understand desperation's role in impatience.* Sometimes desperation can lead us to do things we may regret or would have perhaps not even thought about had the situation been different. Desperation could lead to impulsive behavior. If you are feeling desperate, it could be best to step away from the situation completely, if possible, and choose another course of action. Have you ever felt desperate? Do you feel like there are varying degrees of desperation? Have you ever felt like all options seem like a roadblock? Generally, you can

choose an option that will have the least amount of impact. There might still be fallout or issues, but again, with desperation, it could be very helpful to get another person's thoughts or ideas, seek help, and recognize how damaging impatient, impulsive, or desperate behavior can be in both the short and long terms. Why do you feel desperate? Do you need assistance?

4. *Recognize that patience is for some people a learned skill.* When events like texting and e-mail are so immediate, waiting in real time for someone in front of you at the grocery store can seem like an eternity. Different experiences require different levels of patience. If you weren't born with patience being your best virtue or if you lost it along the way, you may have to spend some time with yourself being aware of what triggers impatience or how you are behaving. If you are always in a rush or losing your patience even in the slightest ways, maybe you need to change your lifestyle in small ways that will have a meaningful impact.

5. *Realize that you can't force or control the future. Don't peek.* Unless you have a time machine that we all don't know about, it would appear that the future unfolds and happens and a fair amount of it is out of our control. When you take actions or behave in ways that go against waiting, then you are responsible fully for absolutely everything you think, do, say, want, need, and so on—but you *do* have a choice to wait. I think about wanting each of my four babies to be born. During those many months of pregnancy, I can remember having to slow my excitement levels down and stay patient with the process. Whether it is pregnancy, writing a book, designing a website, or unveiling a new concept, there is waiting.

6. *Become a little less busy.* This doesn't mean extinguishing your light but rather brilliantly shining it in the right direction, place, and time. Patience is a little more boring than making quick decisions and being impulsive. Patience involves restraint, dealing with delays, and being peaceful with however the future plays out. Patience lacks

drama. It lacks rush and impulse. It also assists in planning or visualization. By becoming a bit less exciting, your light may shine even more brightly and clearly. Your light may assume intention and focus.

7. *Understand that your impatience may hurt others.* Impatience can have a negative impact on others that is often hard to measure. If you feel like your patience is running thin, perhaps pause and don't take any action. Don't say anything and don't do anything. You'll most likely regret words spoken or actions taken when they are not coming from a loving place. Patience is often learned. The following questions will help you discover where your impatience is coming from and help you learn about your behavior. When you are impatient, what part of yourself are you coming from? Are you being vindictive? Are you rushing to do it first? Are you in a place of financial desperation, loss, grief, or despair? Are you really paused and patient and thinking about what you are saying and doing? What is your behavior as a result? Is it light or dark? Is it from your heart or your hurt? Are you going to hurt someone? Are you trampling all over someone to get what you want quickly? Are you realistic?

8. *Put time and patience into perspective.* There are levels of urgency as there are levels of patience. Some moments can't wait. I absolutely wouldn't have wanted the team of doctors saving my life in 1998 to step back and claim, "Patience, everyone. Let's see how this plays out for this young lady." I'm sure they were adequately patient in applying lifesaving techniques and didn't all rush to do the same thing at once, but they did have high urgency levels. I'm also glad they didn't wait it out. So, is your matter life-threatening? Is the matter urgent? Understand that a lack of money or an overdrawn back account is, for example, not generally life-threatening but more of an inconvenience. Waiting in the fast-food line is generally not urgent, nor is standing behind someone in a checkout line who is taking too long. You may feel a sense of urgency and impatience, but the situation itself is nonurgent.

Patience along the way also helps you incorporate a change into your life and to help it become part of your routine. You wake up in the morning and begin to accept the change into your life and all that comes with it. In my case, the day I decided to lose twenty pounds meant I knew I wasn't going to wake up the next day with all twenty pounds gone, despite my wishes. The acceptance came when I made peace with myself to do the work needed to change. Once I did that and implemented small changes, the weight began coming off. I also have made peace with the fact that my body has changed and no longer likes the amount of salt and sugar I was eating previously. I've accepted that.

Think about a time when you wanted something to happen before it could or would actually happen. Think about a date or event in the future. Think about your excitement or anxiety levels with respect to the date or event. Is it something you want to have happen or not have happen? Are you happy, sad, scared, overjoyed? How are you feeling? Between now and then, how are you going to deal with the wait? I think of Christmas and the one year—due to not being able to wait—I peeked at the presents.

The same concept applies to us as adults. Wait it out.

Ask yourself why you are in a rush or why you can't wait. Are you hurting someone with your actions, including maybe yourself? Do you have any alternatives? Can it wait? What's your rush? Some examples I've seen of larger issues at play for people feeling rushed are age, health, and finances. Are any or all real rushes? Urgent? Life-threatening?

Change takes time. A new business takes time. Things must percolate. Percolate your patience also. Patience is wise. Trust the Universe to deliver. Understand that your moments matter—how you spend them and your use of time.

I recently took a poll in my social media accounts. I asked my followers and friends if they would rather have $1 million or 1 million hours. Nearly 100 percent of the 5,000 people who responded said they would rather have

1 million hours. I even increased it to $2 million and kept the same hours and nearly everyone still chose the time.

What would you rather have? How are you spending your time?

Many people say they don't have time to do things, which begs a discussion about time management. Time matters. Time is precious. I know that sounds cliché, but your moments really do matter. Time is not an infinite resource for us each individually. Time marches on, but at some point, *we* stop marching. However, many of us are not consciously structuring our moment-to-moment lives. In fact, a lot of us scratch our head and wonder, *Where did the time go?* It's like looking up at the clock thinking it was just 1 p.m. and it's now 3 PM and you haven't done those two things you needed to get done today. In fact, somehow the list grew longer. Recently I found myself wondering where all the time went as our sons started graduating from college. I went home, looked at pictures of them, and wondered why I hadn't changed a bit and yet they'd all aged by ten years. Baffling.

The answer to managing your time rests with you and no one else. How are you spending your time and energy?

I'm very aware that most of us would rather do just about anything than sit with ourselves and ask ourselves a series of questions aimed at self-improvement. A common reaction to self-help literature is to read something helpful and, with the most permanent of intentions, make the change. Unfortunately, most of the time the change is only temporary, and we revert to our old ways without the proper tools in our bag for actually making life changes. However, the great news is that continual assessment and reassessment of ourselves enable change. Quieting down and doing some soul-searching help you become clear. Chances are, if you've set aside the time to do the work, you are open to and in the process of allowing the discomfort that accompanies growth.

The no-so-great news is that most of us wait until a significant event occurs—usually a wake-up call, often a health crisis—to realize we need to manage our time and energy properly. No, I don't have data to back that up, but if you just stop and look around and live enough life, you see this pattern repeatedly.

You have twenty-four hours in your day. Take that out to 365 days in a year, and let's assume an eighty-year life. Better yet, let's give you a ninety-year life and more hours. Now go easy on me because I'm a self-help guru and not a mathematician, but it looks like in my scenario, you'll have 788,400 hours to live. If you are forty-five—halfway there—you have 394,200 hours to go. How are you going to spend your time?

Now, with my math-magician skills here, let me take some of your time. I'm going to remove 131,400 hours for sleep (eight hours a night for the next forty-five years). That leaves you with 262,800 hours. I'm going to take another 50,000 hours or so for work (no weekends included), leaving you now with 212,800 hours.

I didn't add in hours for school, commutes, exercising, volunteering, vacation, relaxation, eating, and so on, and I took a straight 8-8-8 day— eight hours of sleep, work, and other. Your day might be 4-10-10 or 0-24-0 or 2-12-12 or 6-12-6 or 4-12-8. It just depends on the day and you.

Life nibbles at your time, often without you even really knowing it. This section of the text is intended to get you thinking about your time and energy and realizing that nobody holds your power, energy, time, and decisions but you. We have suggestions and some answers, but those rest in *your* heart—not ours.

What we do know is that eventually you will most likely have a life-changing moment. Unless you can predict the future, you might not see that moment clearly now. For that reason, we should unlearn, undo, and un-multitask often. It then becomes important to constantly relearn and reprioritize. Here are common signs I see in my coaching practice and world of Best Ever You that indicate a need to shift your priorities and manage time better:

- Overall poor health
- Fatigue
- Frequent common colds or flu

- Overweight by more than twenty pounds
- Substance abuse (alcohol, tobacco, drugs, prescription drugs)
- Habitually late, even by five minutes
- Filled with excuses
- Feelings of underappreciation
- Kids and family complaining
- Missing out on moments that matter to others
- Dropping activities you once loved
- Disorganization
- Feeling out of balance
- Exhaustion
- Life-changing illness
- Inflammatory diseases

You bring yourself with you wherever you go. Your goals, values, behaviors, and boundaries go with you at work, home, and play in every hour and every moment.

## TOP 15 WAYS TO HELP MANAGE YOUR TIME AND ENERGY

1. Realize everything isn't a priority. Decide each day what your two most important *personal* and two most important *work-related* priorities are and solidly achieve those in a consistent fashion for six weeks.
2. Say no and say yes, but do them equally and mean both.
3. Understand: You go where you place your energy.
4. Take the time to slow down, teach others, and trust. Mentor, delegate, learn, and ask for help.
5. Be five or more minutes early to everything, both personally and professionally. Account for traffic and the commute, and expect the unexpected.
6. Know where your center of peace is. If you have too much of this or that, learn to bring yourself back to center.
7. Realize you put energy into what is most important to you. Figure

out what is most important to you for real and understand that your moment-to-moment matters most.

8. Manage the five key interrupters: another person's "emergency" or "untimeliness," the phone, e-mail, personal interactions (e.g., the person in your office striking up a conversation), and yourself (mind wandering, procrastination).

9. Understand and live by the principle that you can't undo or get back your time, moments, or energy.

10. Undo.

11. Set time aside.

12. Put your health above all. Without your health intact, not much else matters. Don't wait for a wake-up call.

13. Plan.

14. Volunteer your time. It will help you maintain perspective in many areas of your life.

15. Get very aware. Consider yourself a time management trainee and even get yourself a timer. Retrain yourself and your brain. Get back on track.

So, as we are working toward mastery level in our approach to change, acceptance accompanies great awareness of patience and time and kindness to yourself and others. The goal becomes having the changes become part of you and part of your behavior, without the checklists, reminders, alarms, and so forth. For example, after six months now, I am dairy free, and I get up on my own without an alarm and go for a walk. It's my routine. It's practiced and habitual to the point of morphing into my being.

As we refine and define and perhaps redefine acceptance, please remember to allow. This is where we start to move into mastery—where we accept and allow without falling back into old habits. If you do fall into an old habit or your line of thinking goes back into not accepting things or changes, please know that this is also—in my experience—another moment where change can feel too hard again. Acceptance is a refining point, and your limiting beliefs might still be creeping in. As you push past these feelings and move toward your goals or dreams or the outcome you desire, this is a moment where real transformation happens or we accept our unforeseen circumstance as reality.

As you read these next two accounts, please know they are two incredible stories of overcoming. Neither Kris Fuller nor Deb Landry were given notice to how their lives would change. Their contributions to this book alone speak volumes. Both rose up, faced what was happening, accepted it through this process, and are here to share their hard-earned wisdom.

Let's hear from Kris Fuller first. This is a deeply personal tale about losing her husband, Ben, during the pandemic.

## Stories from the Heart
### Kris M. Fuller—My Beautiful Future

I allow joy, success, beauty, and love into my life. I accept change, hurdles, and aches along the way with grace. My mind-set is strong and guides me toward my beautiful future.

January 2020 started on an incredibly high note. I had just completed a huge and wonderful shift in my career—closing a business and preparing to launch a new chapter where I would focus only on things that served me, helped me grow, enriched my business, and professionally developed me. It was *my* time to shine. I was on fire with ideas, lists of retreats I wanted to attend, new connections and projects, and bookings for my services. My husband, family, and team of supporters were all cheering me on, and I knew it was going to be an incredible year of growth, inspiration, and joy. I was ready to allow success and accept all the wonderful things that were going to flow into my life.

On February 26, however, things changed dramatically. I found myself with my husband, Ben, in Dr. Family's office, waiting to hear news from an ultrasound about his stomach. This excerpt is taken from my blog, Cancer Wife Ninja:

Ben thinks it's gallstones, the doctor thinks it's an ulcer and I'm just annoyed. Annoyed that my husband hasn't been eating, has been in pain and has not been in to see the doctor sooner. It's rare for him to request a doctor visit (in the eight years I have known him, this is the FIRST time ever). The doctor comes in and tries to prepare us with "This is the worst part of my job. Giving bad news to people. And Ben, you are so young. It's not good news." My heart turns to concrete as the next words are shared. It's not the part about Ben having cancer. It's the part about it being stage 4 and already showing up in the liver. It's the part where the doctor looks somber. It's the part where I look across at my husband and see, maybe for the first time, how thin he truly is. His six-foot-two-inch frame is now at 183 pounds.

There is a pit in my stomach. My entire chest hurts. No, it's much more than that. Shoulder to shoulder, it tenses into a pain I have never felt before. Tears come and the doctor passes me the tissue box. I creak out, "What is his life expectancy now?" like a sad robot. What a terrible question. What is wrong with me? Kindly, he replies, "We must wait for the oncologist and more information."

There is a flurry of what's next, what's to come, and how urgent it all is. We leave together, my body is moving through water. I am so heavy with this news and I just want to lie down forever. How quickly my plans to develop, enrich my business, and focus on myself changed!

I'm a mind-set and confidence coach. I believe in the power of positivity and that everyone deserves a beautiful future—no matter what they have gone through. And here I was, faced with my biggest challenge yet. Putting my own words into practice. How was I to accept this news? How could I allow cancer to creep into our lives and simply be here? How could I handle the changes we were about to face, and the uncertainty of it all? The truth is, I could not at first. I was angry, upset, even hurt that the universe could betray me like this. Or was it Ben's body that did the betraying? I resisted allowing, resisted accepting. I fought to have it not be true, but it was futile, of course.

As time went on, I learned—on a crash course—how to care for a stage 4 cancer patient at home. Daily, quickly I had to adjust. And with that, I knew I had to release my anger and put joy into everything we did. Our time was now so precious, how could we waste any of it? I started my day with gratitude, loving things that were precious in my life. Our cat, our home, our yard. The fire-burning stove on our deck that I found comfort in. The time we had together in isolation (we were instructed to keep to ourselves due to Ben's compromised immune system) to talk, watch movies, play games, and simply hang out.

Speaking of isolation, we were also just entering the onset of another hurdle: the beginning of the COVID-19 pandemic. It was surprising how quickly the world shifted into action. I was relieved for our safety and calm, thanks to the leadership we had here in Canada during this time. However, it meant that I was not allowed to accompany Ben to appointments. He received treatments without me, nights alone, and I spent days in the hospital parking lot crying in my car, at a loss. Those were difficult times for both of us. More than anything we wanted to be together. Especially me. I just didn't want him to be alone, ever. Sleepless nights were spent side by side in twin beds—in our living room. My movements were too painful for him to abide and the unfounded reports that sleeping with me is "like sleeping with a small barnyard animal" drove us to the two-bed conclusion. It was a way to be together and some nights we would jest about "having a sleepover" . . . like excited kids at camp.

Looking back, I think the universe had some hand in the timing of my changes. Closing my business created time for me, searching for development opportunities online created new colleagues and projects for me, and caring for the man I loved created a deeper level of understanding and connection between us. Besides caring for Ben (right up until July 16, when he passed away), I cowrote a number-one bestselling Amazon journal with my new partner, Elizabeth Hamilton-Guarino; I published my first young adult adventure book (*Terramara*); I hosted two international online forums; and I completed the renovations on the house Ben and I had started—that's right, I was knee deep in stain and miter saws doing cedar trim, tongue and groove ceilings, and all the finishing touches. Through my grief and heartache, I relied on my daily gratitude practice and exercises for my mind. Daily, I had to reset my thinking and work to find peace.

Of course, I felt anger, sadness, and despair, and I cried a lot in the beginning. And I allowed myself to feel all of those beautiful emotions. I still do. But the choice for me remains: How long do I stay sad? How long do I stay angry? Does it serve me? Processing and feeling my emotions does serve me, of course. We need to feel. It's part of being human. It's important. I believe we all deserve a beautiful future, no matter what we may have done, no matter what we have gone through. That belief propels me forward as I accept my new and different path—as I allow myself to breathe, live, and step each day toward my beautiful future. It's different than I once thought it would be, but I can accept that. I allow a new chapter of my life to be written in a brave, bold way.

● ● ●

As I continue to be with Kris as she navigates, I'm proud to report she is smiling more, crying when she needs to, has moved closer to her family in a beautiful home she just purchased after finishing the renovations on the home she and Ben bought, and more. Here's to her beautiful future.

● ● ●

Next let's chat with Deb Landry. What you'll read from Deb is an incredible story of courage and forgiveness. A humanitarian and philanthropist, Deb specializes in bullying and harassment prevention and safe school climate planning. She has lobbied for legislation in the state of Maine and throughout the United States, serving on ad hoc committees and working as an advocate for children, youth, and teens who are affected by bullying, harassment, or discrimination.

Deb knows firsthand how childhood trauma can psychologically affect the growth of youth and has spent over twenty years as the cofounder and executive director of Crossroads, a youth character education nonprofit with a focus on developmental education to raise resilient and respectful youth.

## Deb Landry—Forgiveness in Acceptance

As a victim of childhood abuse and neglect, I carried a significant amount of baggage into my adult life and relationships. Raised by a mother with borderline personality disorder and antisocial personality disorder, resentment was something I owned and wore proudly and stubbornly. The reality was that I did not have the skills as a child to understand how to let them go, leading to a string of relationships in which I just took what was served, not understanding that I have choices.

Being a child who didn't know the difference between love and abuse was a long road, and ultimately it led to anxiety and depression. Not until I was forty-five years old did I learn a cause and reasons why I had certain feelings and unwarranted beliefs.

No one saw what went on in my private life, and I took that as permission for my mother to parent her way. I didn't see that the parenting or lack thereof was different when others were around because, in the good times, I perched on my branch, waiting for the tree to fall.

When my feelings surfaced, I could break down and understand how forgiveness would set me free. It was not a sacrifice but a way to acceptance, a revelation. Most importantly, the forgiveness wasn't for my mother but for me.

It was hard for me to understand forgiveness, let alone tender it. It made me feel like I was giving in and extending approval by forgiving and forgetting my abuser. In my mind, I didn't want to accept defeat and allow my abuser to continue her unwelcomed behavior. However, carrying guilt, shame, and others' pain led me to a point where it had to go, or I would not survive. Discovering forgiveness meant that revisiting every wound I had from childhood trauma would need individual and specific attention, including understanding.

Accepting that nothing was wrong with me, that my anxiety resulted from my past, I was free to live a stress-free life. I traded in a chaotic childhood that I escaped from and discovered the resources to help reconstruct my life. Facing years of the shame-blame game helped me build my self-esteem and trust while constructing healthy relationships and stronger boundaries.

I embraced that forgiveness would always be a conscious decision. When I let go of my feelings of resentment and pain, I deliberately turned the key to let myself out of my lifelong jail sentence.

By creating intention, I am now better able to protect myself from those who cause me hurt. The stability within relationships, the trust I have in my friends and family, and the strength I have found in myself may have been a long time coming, but well worth the wait.

When I think about a day when I was seven years old, standing in the street searching for a sense of belonging, I can still feel the penetrating desire to escape and run that I felt that day so long ago. At the time, I couldn't understand why I felt such a strong need to break away—but now I know why. Sixty years have given me the insight, the answers, and understanding of what I was feeling. I still wonder how my child's brain was able to formulate such mysterious thoughts. I can only conclude it was all due to undertaking a job I didn't know I applied for: the position of fulfilling the role of a parent in a relationship with a psychologically and emotionally abusive mother who was a covert narcissist.

I took these steps by self-love, letting go of resentment, asking for professional help, and most of all, being kind to myself. It wasn't easy, but I learned that forgiveness was never for my abusers during this process. They didn't ask for it, and it was not for me to judge, let alone evaluate or criticize others. I learned that blaming and passing judgment only stifled my personal growth and well-being. Carrying guilt instead of love and forgiveness was killing my mental health. I want people to know that most abuse is subtle and hidden, not dramatized like in books or movies.

People handle trauma, secrets, and abuse in various ways. My way enabled me to find the root of my pain through forgiveness. This uncomfortable process healed my emotional wounds, confirming how necessary the forgiveness journey is to lead to recovery.

● ● ●

These are both deeply touching stories, and again I am so proud of both Kris and Deb for being so brave and sharing them with us. We all learn from one another and heal in our own different ways.

## POINTS TO PONDER

Think. Write. Talk. Action. *(Because practice makes us our best.)*

### EXERCISE 13: What's Your Rush?

1. In a separate journal or below, write down five circumstances that bother you and cause you to become impatient. For each of them, ask yourself why you are impatient then. Do you know why?

_____

_____

_____

_____

_____

2. How do you accept things and still crave change?

_____

3. Are you tolerant? _____

4. Think of five ways you think you could be more patient in each of the circumstances that you wrote down for the first question. For example, if

you are in a long line and feel yourself getting impatient, what could you do? Catch yourself in your scenarios and behave in a way that is more loving to all involved.

_____

_____

_____

_____

_____

5. **The next time you are at the grocery store with fifteen items or less in your cart, intentionally place yourself behind the person with one or two carts filled. Stand patiently behind them. Maybe even ask them if they need a hand. Do this a few times, until you don't feel like you have to rush through the express lane.**

Apply the concepts of this point in your life in other situations where waiting is required. This could be a doctor's office, traffic, a fast-food line, a restaurant, and so on. When you start to wonder, *What is taking so long?* ask yourself, *Is it really them? Or is it me?* Could they be a little speedier but are doing their best? Are you in a rush and perceiving that everyone else is slow and in your way?

6. **Slow yourself down. Pick an activity that you normally rush through and intentionally slow yourself down. Did you do things differently? Did you see anything new?**

_____

7. **In a separate journal or below, list up to ten things you need to get done or want to do in your life. Now rank them in order of importance. Is anything completely urgent? On another page, list ten everyday types of situations where you could be more patient with people. Can you apply time and meaningful choices to the matters?**

_____

_____

_____

_____

_____

_____

_____

_____

_____

_____

## EXERCISE 14: How Much Time Do You Have?

1. Write your key thoughts on how you currently use your time and how you wish you used your time.

How I Currently Use My Time

How I Wish I Would Use My Time

_____     _____

_____     _____

_____     _____

_____     _____

_____     _____

2. Referring to the Top 15 Ways list earlier in the chapter, do you have any signs of time management issues? Be honest with yourself.

_____

_____

3. Write down three to five ways you feel you could manage your time better.

_____

_____

_____

_____

_____

4. Would you rather have 1 million hours or $1 million? Why?

_____

_____

_____

# PART 3

# ALIGN YOUR ENERGY

CHAPTER 8
# ENGAGE

*In our eighth point, we gather and give back. In this point, we start to find community and like-minded folks. This is a huge part of change, as surrounding ourselves with the proper people fosters peace and puts everything we want to change in motion. If we can't surround ourselves ideally, then we need to have the tools to separate ourselves based on our values, goals, beliefs, and behavior and to recognize naysayers.*

**I'm starting this chapter out** with one of my favorite success tips.

## SUCCESS TIP #28: Instead of Asking, "What's in It for Me?" Ask, "What's in It for Us?"

Together we create the energy needed for change. Your positive energy fuels humanity, and we can create waves of peace. Also, each person you meet teaches you something, and you will also teach them something. You create change. We create change, and how you treat people tells all. Each day is filled with more moments to love one another and opportunities to pay closer attention to one another. We all need one another.

If you listen closely, you'll hear humanity crying for compassion.

## SUCCESS TIP #29: People Remember How You Made Them Feel More Than What You Said

I know you can't control how you make people feel, but they will remember how they feel from interacting with you. I just had this happen to me with four people who were so busy they couldn't make time for me. Well, we all know how that feels. It makes you feel, if you allow it to, less important or of no significance to the other person. People make time for what is important to them. You do it, too, so also be aware of how you make others feel when you don't make time for them properly or don't have a compassionate response as to why you are unable to do whatever it is.

Remember that most people are going about their daily life with at least one major concern playing in the background, usually related to health or illness, monetary stress, bad relationships, grief, and sometimes all of them. Often we meet others who have been so demoralized that they question our attempts at giving them positive energy. Many live their lives feeling like they are schoolchildren alone at the lunch table. They feel excluded, alone, neglected, unheard, isolated, mistreated, misunderstood, and more.

## SUCCESS TIP #30: It's Up to All of Us to Pay Closer Attention to One Another

Paying much closer attention is the start and a step forward to being present, accepting, inclusive, and loving others. How are your relationships with other people? If you encounter negativity, apply more love and more positive energy.

## SUCCESS TIP #31: Treat Another Person's Heart as if It Is Your Own

In our eighth point, we find community and like-minded folks who perhaps have had the same experiences or have put on enough mileage to have some thoughts, advice, ideas, or direction for us. Maybe this is you engaging others. This is a huge part of change, as surrounding ourselves with the proper people fosters peace and puts in motion everything we want to change. If we surround ourselves ideally, then we have the tools to separate ourselves based on our values, goals, beliefs, and behavior and recognize naysayers. We find leadership, even if that leadership is internal to us and how we guide ourselves in our own moments. You go where you place your energy. Search for peace. Do more of what makes you peaceful. Find your joy. Find your peace and the people who surround those findings.

Speaking of world-class energy, as we engage others or others engage us, you'll notice that you just can't quite put your finger on some things, like that certain something that demonstrates excellence. It's a way people carry themselves or a quality that can't be measured. Yet the best of the best also pay attention to those things that matter most. How you treat people most likely will be how you are remembered more than any action, award, or event.

In working with people, I've developed the Five Intangibles. People operating with the Five Intangibles have five distinct ways they go about life naturally; often they are just this way.

## THE FIVE INTANGIBLES

**Drive:** Belief in discovering the power of motivation, competition, growth, goals, will, and purpose.

**Trust:** Belief in character, behavior, values, beliefs, choices, awareness, reliability, and integrity, all combining to allow others to place their trust in you and you in them.

**Adaptability:** Belief that anything is possible based on your ability to maneuver and your mind-set being open, particularly to change and new ideas. This involves listening to suggestions and other people often, as well as trusting yourself and taking risks.

**Perseverance:** Belief in the incredible power of healing, adaptability, strength, growth, purpose, and forgiveness.

**Leadership:** Belief that you are always following, leading, and learning. Careful consideration to body language, character, perseverance, trust, drive, adaptability, wisdom, humor, connectedness, purpose, and community are present in leadership.

When a person with one or more of these intangibles engages you, you know you are around excellence. It is a vibe and a way they conduct themselves without arrogance. They do not make you feel small or less than, but rather they make you feel on top of the world and included.

I was recently on a Zoom call with Dr. Ivan Misner who is the founder and Chief Visionary Officer of BNI (Business Network International). BNI is a multimillion-dollar company with hundreds of thousands of members globally. BNI is the world's leading business referral organization, with over 280,000 members in more than 10,000 BNI chapters worldwide. In 2020 alone, BNI members shared over 11.5 million valuable new client referrals and generated over $16.2 billion in revenue.

As we were chatting, he was talking about an article he needed to send me for BestEverYou.com, and as kind and humble as he is, he went into his own e-mail and on the spot sent it to me. It's July 2021's post on the site. He then went on to add, "I love writing for your website." How kind and sweet is he? He has plenty of assistants and employees who could be sending me his articles for the website, and yet each month they come directly from Ivan.

So as Ivan encounters all he meets with his world-class energy of kindness, incredible presence, and follow-through, his example is an important reminder to celebrate, accept, and always be mindful and conscious of what makes you become your Best Ever You, as when you engage others it will be with that sense of peace and those intangibles.

This is an important moment to think about how you are engaging others. What is your outward energy to other people? What are you like? If you met you in the grocery store, on the baseball field, or in a yoga class, a hospital, a classroom, and so forth, what type of person would you like to meet? Would we like to engage you? What are your leadership skills like, even if you aren't leading? Is your energy happy? Sad? Mopey? Fun? What is it like to be around you? What are your moods like? Are you constantly cracking jokes and being sarcastic? What is it like when you are mad? I know that's a lot to think about, but really, what are you like? The inner you: Who is that?

Every now and then I run into people I find pretty much impossible for me to engage. Here is a story about Joel. Joel came to me many years back after his first heart attack, asking for my help. I knew instantly that I needed to refer Joel to a therapist as Joel wasn't wanting to move forward. He was stuck in the past and not ready or willing to accept his present situation. He couldn't accept who he had become. Joel had gained over 120 pounds and was formerly an incredible athlete. Through an injury and now a heart attack, Joel couldn't find peace in the physical changes. Joel said to me, "Well, I used to be able to run ten miles with ease and now I can barely walk up the street." To add to this, Joel was festering mad. He was so angry that I knew I couldn't work with him. He rocked my peace to the core. I often wonder about Joel, but here is my point. You don't have to fully engage with every person you meet, and you aren't going to be everyone's cup of tea and they aren't going to be yours. People pleasers, beware.

It was in Joel's best interest and mine to move along. However, I did treat Joel with kindness and respect, and gave him a beautiful referral.

## SUCCESS TIP #32: Some People Aren't for You, and You Aren't for Them; Know and Use Your Boundaries

How often do you engage others in meaningful conversations? A moment with another person when you are listening and not talking so much can be so meaningful and pivotal. Are you a good listener? I had a moment with my mom that I'd like to share with you. I hope you'll be a good listener as I tell you this because it's a moment I'll never forget, and I hope you find a moment like this with your loved ones.

● ● ●

After my dad passed away and a few weeks before her own surgery in 2019, my mom wanted to go to Walmart to get some things for surgery. Of all her children, I was the one who didn't have little kids and could be by her side 24/7. So I left Maine and went to Minnesota. Now, whenever you return home, or at least when I do anyway, I feel like I go back to being a little kid. There are some things from home that are just home. This time, however, didn't feel that way at all. I felt like an adult taking care of an adult. My mom needed help.

So there we were. We arrived at the Walmart parking lot and it began to rain. It was pouring. Absolutely pouring, so much so that it wasn't that great driving back home either, so we decided to stay put. My mom and I decided to stay in the car and have a chat. I was talking about closing the Best Ever You Network. Well, I have two yellow notebooks of all her suggestions for the company. Trust me, she's a brilliant businessperson, so she had some amazing ideas. We were on topics like change, jealousy, and anger.

Then we came to weight loss, probably our all-time favorite thing to chat about. I said, "You know, we wear in public what we eat in private." She looked at me like I'd said something profound as if it was the weight loss cure-all and she said, "That needs to go in your next book." (Done!) As the rain started to calm down, I said, "Let's write down everything you need me to do for you, things you need to buy, and then anything else you are thinking of in case something happens with this surgery."

We had a conversation about everything, and it comes to the part about if something terrible should happen.

She said, "I already have a will."

And I said, "Okay, well then, let me ask you all sorts of stuff I've never asked you in case something really does happen." She proceeded to tell me the what and where and why. I agreed; we had discussed doing a will before. I was reminded.

I said, "No, the important stuff, like stuff I didn't ask about Dad and you. Tell me a story about something I don't know about you."

We were talking and it was all about how challenging it could be to take care of Dad and work while in your sixties and seventies. She talked about how expensive medication was and care and just the stress and worry with someone that ill for so long and how magnificent Dad was. It was a difficult situation to navigate, but she had no regrets and was very positive, just as my mom always is. She let me know she had his care and the expense in hand. Also that my brothers and sisters were there, and we all covered any shortfalls.

I began to talk about the move from one house to the second house, which was a beautiful and peaceful lakefront home.

I was recalling and telling her how neat I thought that house was, and she proceeded to tell me that the whole time they were living there they felt like they were secretly less than everyone else in the neighborhood. My mom said she was jealous of yards, flowers, clothes, barbecues, and whatever else you could be jealous of while living in a lakefront mansion with one income. That was, until one day a neighbor lady knocked on her door. She was bringing over something to give to my mom. My mom and the lady got to chatting and my mom said how stunning her yard was and how beautiful the house looked and was full of jealous compliments, but they were kind.

The neighbor did something my mom never, ever expected. She proceeded to break down and cry. My mom's ears and heart and soul then heard all about how their perfect neighbors were actually in the final stages of divorce and foreclosure, and how they had fixed their house up with final money for their daughter's wedding this weekend, which was completely for show before they let their four adult children know they were being foreclosed on. They had, in their minds, concluded with a stab at perfection: their youngest child's fairytale, childhood marriage.

My mom said to me, "I had absolutely no idea all of this was going on with her and she had absolutely no idea anything was going on with Dad recovering from a stroke. We had everything and all appearances from the outside looking in, perfect. Scratch a bit below the surface, and you'll find everything." She confessed she had been watching my mother care for her flowers and dogs and longed for the days when her family all came for Sunday dinner and just dropped in.

It was a moment when my mom said she stopped being jealous of anyone ever again and it happened at age sixty-five and she learned to ask for help. They also downsized to match their new reality and upgraded to match their soul.

That was a moment I'll never forget.

We both agreed that you absolutely can't tell what is really happening in another person's life, so treat all you encounter with a sense of grace, elegance, compassion, and collaboration, as we are all in this together. My mother taught me that. Have those intangibles going at all moments.

Ask friends and family these two things: Tell me something I don't know about you. Tell me something about your life story.

So often we are afraid to engage others for fear they might discover what is really going on. We may feel embarrassed to tell or share the truth.

Are you sharing your truths and finding like-minded people or people who have had similar experiences to yours? Are you part of a community, online or otherwise? Now, this isn't a sales pitch for my network, as it is completely free to join, but we'd love to have you as a member at the Best Ever You Network (BestEverYou.com). I promise you a network full of people who will engage and accept you. We are a very inclusive network.

As you read these next two accounts, please realize they are two incredible stories of engaging others. Eleanor Garrow-Holding and Sarah Cronk both build community around causes they care about.

## Stories from the Heart
### Eleanor Garrow-Holding—Creating Community

December 5 is a date I will never forget. It is the day my father was laid to rest in 2004. And it is the day my son had an anaphylactic reaction to pecans in 2005.

Thomas was just nineteen months old, and I thought I was going to lose him.

We were attending a family birthday party and had no reason to believe Thomas might have an issue with food at the party. He'd never had an allergic reaction before. Surrounded by family (and five months' pregnant with my daughter, Anne), I felt comfortable letting Thomas explore the party and the food table. He took one bite of an English toffee bar with crushed pecans, and within thirty seconds he was coughing, and his face was covered in hives. Something was very wrong.

My cousin, a hospital administrator, called ahead and told the hospital staff what Thomas had eaten and the symptoms he was having while my mom drove us two miles to the hospital. The Emergency Department team was waiting outside.

In the seven minutes it took to drive to the Emergency Department entrance, Thomas had become completely unrecognizable to me. He was covered in hives from head to toe. His eyes were now swollen shut. His lips were swollen, and he was coughing and gasping for air. A doctor took him from my arms and laid his small body on a hospital gurney.

Emergency Department staff gave Thomas three doses of epinephrine plus an antihistamine and steroids. They hooked him up to heart and lung monitors and gave him an oxygen mask. About three hours later, Thomas started to look himself again. Doctors admitted him to the pediatric unit for overnight observation to ensure Thomas did not have a second allergic reaction (biphasic), which further frightened me.

I had so many questions and worries going through my head. What is happening? We have no family history of food allergy! Is my new baby going to have food allergies, too? I knew nothing about food allergies despite my background in healthcare administration. Nobody I knew had food allergies or a child with food allergies. I was beyond scared and felt so alone.

Thankfully, Thomas had a restful night. He was discharged the next day, and we were told to visit our pediatrician for a prescription for an epinephrine auto-injector and then make an appointment to see a board-certified allergist for allergy testing and accurate diagnosis. Next, I called Lurie Children's Hospital of Chicago to schedule an appointment for allergy testing and diagnosis. Thomas tested positive for all tree nuts, peanut, and sesame.

I learned that we were *not* alone in this new world of food allergies. Many food allergy support groups are around Chicago but none were in our area, so I started educating myself and my family about food allergies and anaphylaxis. I resigned from my job because I did not trust anyone to care for Thomas. I traveled to attend support group meetings and meet other food allergy parents. I met amazing people who mentored, educated, and supported me during my food allergy journey. My mom, a registered nurse, was our biggest supporter.

I started a food allergy support group in the county where I lived. Families really needed that support. Meetings were in person with expert guest speakers. We gave parents educational materials, samples from allergen-friendly food companies, and epinephrine trainers. Parents loved socializing with families that shared the same life experiences. And I had found my passion—educating food allergy families and giving back to this special community.

We had our ups and downs in those early days, including incidents of food allergy bullying in school, but I was not going to let fear take over—or allow anyone to instill fear in us! I would not let food allergies define Thomas or hold us back from living life, and I wanted every family to have that same opportunity. It's all about the education! That's what inspired me to help families across the country by forming the Food Allergy and Anaphylaxis Connection Team (FAACT).

For every challenge we faced, I knew thousands of other families were going through the same thing. No one should have to make this food allergy journey alone. FAACT's mission is beyond education—it's about helping families advocate for their children's rights and best lives, from the classroom to the athletic field, sleepovers to holiday family dinners.

The FAACT team includes a lawyer who helps families fight for their children's civil rights and a school psychologist who provides mental health education. We have team members spearheading diversity initiatives and outreach to underserved communities of color, working with local advocates to pass legislation, and growing the community of support groups for people with food allergies. Every person on our team shares a passion for creating community and engaging that community for the common good.

I taught Thomas how to advocate for himself at a young age, and he has always been his own best advocate. I am so proud of him! I also taught our daughter, Anne, to be an advocate for Thomas and other children with food allergies—and for herself. When one member of the family has food allergies, it affects the entire family.

To educate and engage the whole family, I created Camp TAG (The Allergy Gang), a summer day camp for children with food allergies, eosinophilic disorders or other chronic immune system disorders, celiac disease, food protein-induced enterocolitis syndrome (FPIES), asthma, and their nonallergic siblings to enjoy camp together, which is operated under FAACT's umbrella. We also host an annual teen retreat to bring together teens with food allergies, their nonallergic siblings, and their parents, with age-appropriate content and plenty of time to create lasting connections.

Thomas stayed in school and graduated high school this spring. He did this while going through numerous oral food challenges, endoscopies (for eosinophilic esophagitis, thankfully now in remission), food reintroductions, and skin/blood tests. Thomas outgrew his allergy to peanut, sesame, and almond. We still have to avoid all tree nuts.

My message to food allergy families is that you are not alone. Whether you are newly diagnosed or a longtime member of the allergy community, FAACT is your home for education, advocacy, and connections with other parents and adults affected by food allergies and life-threatening anaphylaxis. FAACT is here to support you today, tomorrow, and into the future. These connections keep me going every day, knowing that there are always going to be new families facing new food allergy challenges.

I thank God every day for my family's support and for the help of many others in the food allergy community. I thank God and my dad for watching over Thomas on that fateful December 5. We are all in this together.

● ● ●

I have had the pleasure of working closely with Eleanor with our shared cause of food allergy awareness. I share her goal of keeping us alive and thriving with food allergies and am so thankful her organization exists. It helps people of all ages, all over the world, feel confident and informed.

Next, let's meet Sarah Cronk. *The Best Ever You Show* and the Best Ever You Network were both big supporters of Sarah as a teenager when she first started her nonprofit Generation Spirit (formerly The Sparkle Effect). It's been wonderful to watch Sarah over the years evolve into who she is today and will be moving forward.

## Sarah Cronk—Simple Invitations

When I was little, my family home (a 1970s era split-level on a quiet court in Iowa) looked normal—until you stepped inside. Instead of a living room, we had a classroom. Posters lined the walls, books and flashcards filled the shelves, and a bulky video camera perched expectantly on its tripod in the corner. In place of a dining room, we had what we called "Command Central." There, my parents conducted weekly meetings with a team of therapists (young, enthusiastic women recruited from two local colleges) who rotated in and out of our home. In every other room, labels quelled any confusion about the basic functions of our everyday appliances: "This is a refrigerator. It keeps food cold." My family home doubled as a center for applied behavioral analysis—a full-time program and support system for my older brother Charlie, who is on the autism spectrum.

Our home and our lives weren't "normal"—at least not to those looking in—but my childhood was nevertheless a happy one. Because Charlie's therapy primarily focused on developing social skills, I—along with several neighborhood kids—were routinely invited to take part. During the summer months when Charlie and I were in elementary school, our family hosted "Rain or Shine," a makeshift summer school led by Charlie's therapists, where neighborhood friends came together in our basement for games, activities, and snacks. Our house was usually brimming with young people having fun together.

The family's quest to ensure Charlie's maximum participation and inclusion at home, in school, and in extracurricular activities was woven into our everyday existence. For several years, the formula we created worked. Charlie's growth and social development exceeded everyone's expectations and we were all relatively happy. Over time, however, as Charlie and I grew older and entered junior high, creating socially inclusive opportunities proved to be more challenging. It's one thing to enroll elementary-age peers in playdates and therapy sessions. It's another to attempt to orchestrate friendships for a teenager. By the time we entered high school, social inclusion had become elusive.

Charlie is extremely smart, and with a few accommodations he handled the academic demands of high school without much trouble. The social demands, on the other hand, were proving insurmountable. The lunch period was the worst. Every day, I watched as Charlie was politely turned away from table after table. Eventually, he would take his tray into the nurse's office and eat alone. Eventually, he stopped wanting to go to school. My parents—historically so able to create whatever Charlie needed—were at a complete loss. As a family, we were flailing.

Then something unexpected happened. A popular upperclassman on the swim team, Jared, invited Charlie to sit at his lunch table. Within weeks, Jared convinced Charlie to join the high school swim team. Those two simple invitations (issued with no prompting or encouragement from us) gave Charlie a place to belong and people to belong to.

Our family did what any grateful family would do. We thanked Jared over and over and over again. To me, the repeated expressions of gratitude started to feel like a closed loop—like an ending instead of a beginning. Then, it hit me: instead of repeatedly thanking Jared, I should emulate him. After all, like Jared, I was fully capable of extending simple invitations.

That's what I did. A cheerleader at the time, I created a new cheer team at my school and invited students with disabilities to join. Our team, the Pleasant Valley High School Spartan Sparkles of Bettendorf, Iowa, had humble beginnings. Five students with disabilities ranging from Down syndrome to autism and five students without disabilities cheered on the Pleasant Valley Spartans at home football and basketball games.

Within a few months, our roster overflowed, we had a waiting list, and families were relocating into our district in hopes of securing a spot for their child on the team. All this from a simple invitation: "Yes, we want *you*. Please join."

I knew it was time to think bigger. It was time to bring my idea to schools and students outside Iowa, to start extending more invitations. In 2009, at fifteen years old, I started Generation Spirit, a national nonprofit organization dedicated to creating and tangibly supporting inclusive spirit teams in schools nationwide. I set a goal of generating 100 new teams.

Once again, the family dining room became Command Central, but this time for a new purpose. Armed with only a ream of Generation Spirit letterhead and the unbridled audacity of a teen on a mission, I penned letters to one hundred schools inviting them to get involved. I wrote to national media outlets, inviting them to share our story. I wrote to CEOs of companies I admired, inviting them to counsel me on my journey.

Within six months, I received a few invitations in return. I was invited to appear on *ABC World News*, in *People* magazine, and on *The Oprah Winfrey Show*. I was asked to partner with the largest cheerleading company in the world. I started receiving invites from schools to start new teams and teach more students about the power of inclusion.

Most importantly, more than ten years later, Generation Spirit has built a community of over 225 inclusive spirit teams across thirty-one states. More than 20,000 students with and without disabilities have participated on our teams. Over the years, our teams have helped schools reshape their culture to one where every member feels valued and celebrated, not in spite of but because of their differences. We've created communities where showing up for each other becomes the norm and connection is valued over perfection.

As for me? My purpose remains clear: to issue simple invitations to a world where we celebrate our uniqueness alongside our shared humanity.

● ● ●

"Shared humanity." The best phrase ever. What did you learn from Eleanor and Sarah? Both of their stories remind us of how we can elevate others. As we each do our part, we elevate humanity. It is up to each of us to stop and pause. You have the opportunity to practice gratitude in each and every moment.

In Exercises 15 and 16, we are going to reflect on who you are and who is around you.

## POINTS TO PONDER

Think. Write. Talk. Action. *(Because practice makes us our best.)*

### EXERCISE 15: Find Your Network, Community, and Resources

1. How do you like to engage others?

_____

2. What is an area of expertise where you can give back?

_____

3. What story about yourself, like those in this book, could you share with others?

_____

4. Who is in your current circle?

_____

5. Who do you know?

_____

6. Who needs to know you?

_____

7. Who do you want to know?

_____

8. **Perform one random act of kindness for someone else.** If you do this, please join our Percolate Project Group on Facebook.

## EXERCISE 16: Your Story

**Write a few short paragraphs about yourself.**

_____

_____

_____

_____

_____

_____

_____

_____

_____

_____

_____

_____

_____

_____

_____

_____

_____

_____

_____

_____

_____

_____

_____

# CHAPTER 9
# MASTER

*For the ninth point, we enter a mastery level, as we can now recognize how to expand on the concept of understanding and bring ourselves back to peace and all the core principles of being our best.*

*Routine practice and the highest, best self-mastery are present to ourselves and all we encounter. We have a sense of You, Me, Us, and We and we encounter others with a sense of gratitude, compassion, and collaboration. We are mastering awareness and self-discipline, where our moments matter. We are not rushed, and we have the ability to balance. We become our Best Ever You and are our highest, most peaceful self, regardless of anything and everything.*

**So know that as of right now,** I want to throw you a light saber and tell you to "Think Jedi" here in our ninth point of change, when we become Change Masters. You're on your way to being really aware of others and how we all make and process change. You've shown that you can know the process to make change or adapt to an unforeseen circumstance.

By the time we've reached mastery level at any endeavor, we have perhaps logged in thousands of hours or are working on goals to do so and aligned our energy to become masterful at what we want to do or in adjusting to our circumstance. You may have been called upon to help others. As we continue to become our best, remember: You can be confident without arrogance. You can be successful and remain humble. You can be accepted without sacrificing your values. You can be uncomfortable to change and grow. You can be wise and be open to learning from others. You can be a great listener and still be heard.

As we continue, we discover this may be something we want to teach others to do. At this point we have learned not only much of the process of change, but we can now recognize how to expand our concept of understanding and how to bring ourselves back to peace and all the core principles of being our best. Routine practice and highest, best self-mastery are present to us and all we encounter. We have a sense of You, Me, Us, and We, and we encounter others with a sense of gratitude, compassion, and collaboration. We are mastering awareness and self-discipline, where our moments matter. We are not rushed, and we have the ability to balance. We become our Best Ever You and are our highest, most peaceful self, regardless of anything and everything.

I'd like to think that you can be a master of change at any age or for anyone. In fact, sometimes those younger than us or different from us are the wisest teachers. When we make room for what we all have to offer, we become even better.

One thing I see a lot of is people who have a message but appear silenced on a variety of levels because they don't feel like they are the be-all and end-all expert on the topic. For example, I felt that way *big time* when I first started the Best Ever You Network. I remember walking in from my job that I had just decided to move forward from and letting my husband and children know that I had written a business plan for the Best Ever

You Network in my office that day. Next, I remember walking up to my neighbor's house and securing a domain and really knowing nothing about websites or domains in the context of being a designer or website developer and running a business around it. Over the past many years now, I have leaned on others with more expertise than I have in a variety of topics, not only to learn but to grow our network. The purpose is to provide materials, classes, and more in personal and professional development that help us all be our best, most successful selves. We help people get results. We chart a course together, we do a lot of work, and we hold ourselves accountable.

I've had plenty of limiting beliefs along the way and have had to learn to quiet any negative chatter. I do this with a two-part system that I call the Gratitude Flip. It is how you turn your inner critic into your best friend and love yourself. It is how you quiet all the negative self-talk and turn it into successful brain speak.

## SUCCESS TIP #33: Use the Gratitude Flip to Find Perspective

As soon as you find yourself talking negatively, *stop*. It is low-energy activity and you need to sustain positive energy, grounded in gratitude, self-talk, and love. This is where "I can't" becomes "I can," with the twist of a thought. You've applied love. You've got this. Success starts here, when you turn your limiting beliefs upside down and apply love. This also helps you maintain perspective on what is really important.

I believe that recognizing that this is happening and learning to train your brain to think positively and take the positive outcome path are some of the biggest obstacles to success and a direct path to failure if you aren't aware. They are critical steps in mastery. As with mastery and having an impact on other people, you may have to put yourself out there a bit: writing a book, giving a speech, or conducting a class.

My point in sharing that with you is that maybe when it feels like it's time to quit or you are second-guessing yourself, it's actually time to strengthen your mind-set, work harder, and adopt a never-give-up approach. As you sort through your feelings, you may discover that those around you may have impacted you in a negative way.

I'll never forgot the time, just shortly after I registered besteveryou.com, that someone wanted the domain. They called and called and called to get me to give it up. I struck a nerve with a very nasty guy who proceeded to call me "a washed-up, old, soccer mom who would never ever ever go anywhere in life but down and I should go get a real job." Whoa. I am very proud of my response, which was, "Our kids don't even play soccer." And I hung up. It was my way of saying you don't know me and then I remember doubling down and thinking, *Oh, I might have something here.* I went and registered the domain for ten more years.

After, I remember thinking, *OMG, I can't unhear that. What in the world am I going to do to get that out of my head, out of my thinking?* I'm rather an empath of sorts in reality, so I'm going to hang on to that. I thought so much about it, and I asked my husband if I was being ridiculous. I began to second-and third guess myself. In fact, I asked everyone if I was being ridiculous with my new company idea. This was a stranger, and this was before free-flowing negative remarks flooded comment fields, tweets, and so forth. I'm so glad I charged ahead.

I'm sharing this with you as we all have a lot to master. Be kind to yourself and be kind to others. That's really the contest to have with one another—who is the kindest? By the way, who is the kindest person you know? Give them a call or a hug and let them know. It's another great hashtag social media moment. Let me know who that person is and please use the #ChangeGuidebook. The world needs them.

Instead, I've used it as a story that has helped shape who I am today. Who are you? Let's think about that for a moment. I'd like to introduce you to a success tip I use called Your Statement of Personal Power.

## SUCCESS TIP #34: Write and Use Your Statement of Personal Power

If you don't already have one, this is a moment to design a fifteen- to forty-five-second statement about who you are and what you do. For example, when someone asks, "What do you do?" instead of stumbling, you have a statement of personal power. "My name is Elizabeth, and I make the best chocolate chip cookies you'll ever taste." I know without fail, this is something I can do. It's also a conversation starter and usually leads to either a giveaway, donation, or a sale. At one point in our lives, my cookies were welcome packages. Real estate agents gave them as thank-you gifts to buyers of just-sold homes.

● ● ●

These next two folks are smart cookies, and I'm honored they both said yes to including their stories within these pages. They occupy my heart and mind often, both leaders who have achieved mastery in their professional fields.

## Stories from the Heart
### Ivan Misner—Ivan's Why

Who's in your story? There has probably been someone in your life—a coach, grandparent, teacher, aunt, or spiritual mentor—who's made a difference for you. It may have been when you were young (it generally is) or it may have been recently. It may have been a positive experience, or it may have been very negative. Either way, it is your "why" for what you have become in life.

I've certainly had people who have made a significant difference in my life. One of those people was my freshman high school teacher, Mr. Romero, at Gladstone High School in southern California. Mr. Romero taught history, and that class was the one that selected the student council representative for the freshmen. I had run for student council numerous times in junior high school and was soundly defeated each time. The elections weren't even remotely close. In fact, I came in dead last every time. Each election was a humiliating experience that left an indelible impression on me. So, by the time high school rolled around, I had no intention of running for student council again. *Ever!*

The first week of freshman history class, our teacher, Mr. Romero, asked all the students, "Because we pick the freshman student council representative from this year's history class, are there any volunteers for the position? Who would like to do it?" Nobody volunteered. Finally one of the prettiest, most popular girls in the class said, "Oh, Mr. Romero, you know, I would do it, but I'm just so busy! I don't have the time to do something like that."

Mr. Romero replied, "That's okay, you don't have to do it. But if no one's interested in volunteering, as the teacher, I get to pick. Are you okay with that?"

The students came back with cheers: "Yeah, yeah, yeah—you go ahead and pick!" So the teacher looked around the class, paused his gaze at me, and, looking me straight in the eyes, he said, "Ivan, I'll bet you would love to do this, wouldn't you?"

I replied, "Well, um, well, yeah, I kind of would, Mr. Romero." My momentary elation was immediately squashed when the entire class, almost in unison, moaned, "Oh, no. Not Ivan!" Even the too-busy popular girl stood up and said, "No, no, Mr. Romero. You know what—I'm actually not that busy. If you're going to pick Ivan, I can do it after all!" Of course, while she was saying all this, I was thinking, *Hello. You all see me sitting here, right?* But I couldn't actually open my mouth to speak. I just sat there, quiet and embarrassed, holding my breath. Have you ever had a moment like this? When you felt so small you just wanted to slip underneath the carpet? That was how I felt in that moment.

It's important to put this experience in context. Today, I'm an author, speaker, and fairly successful businessman with franchises on every populated continent of the world. But remember, this was happening to me as a young thirteen-year-old boy. I lacked confidence, I felt like I didn't fit in at all, and I couldn't get a chance to prove myself at something I really wanted to do. Just imagine, for a moment, how humiliating this was for me. I didn't have the advantage of peeking into the future to know where I would end up. I have to tell you, it was a raw, exposed moment.

Somehow, Mr. Romero understood that, and he gave the ever-popular girl a withering look and said, "No, you had your chance to volunteer, and you didn't take it. So I'm empowered to pick a representative, and I pick Ivan. He's the student representative! Now, open your books and turn to Chapter 2."

Despite the grumbles rolling through the classroom, Mr. Romero's decision was final. I was the Student Council Representative. My teacher believed that I could do a good job. I took a deep breath in and knew I would work hard—really hard—to prove him right. When the year-end Student Council elections came around for the following year, I decided to do something I had vowed to never do again: I ran for Student Council. That same class who loudly protested my appointment voted me in for another year, by a landslide! As a matter of fact, I won every election in high school after that—Student Council, Activities Director, Student Body President— every single one.

It all started with Mr. Romero seeing something in me that I had not been able to see in myself. His giving me that chance allowed me to prove myself. This infused confidence in me, and that made a huge difference in my life. I gained leadership skills and learned responsibility by being involved in those school projects that I had to take from the beginning to the end. Mr. Romero positively influenced my life by giving me the *opportunity* to succeed. He didn't do the hard work for me, but he opened the door for me. He gave me a chance to excel, to succeed, and to show what I was capable of doing.

Years later, I knew this was an important experience in my life, but I never realized how seminal it truly was to the man that I would become. It wasn't until about ten years ago at an Asentiv seminar where we were all studying our Emotionally Charged Connections (ECCs) to understand why we do what we do that I came to realize that my entire life's work was in fact, a reflection of what Mr. Romero did for me as a young man.

Every book I've written or business I've started has been an attempt to give other people an *opportunity* to succeed, to excel, and to accomplish what they want to accomplish in life. I can't "make" someone successful. Only they can do that. I can, however, provide the system, the process, and the *opportunity* for them to achieve their dreams. I have been continuously reliving what Mr. Romero did for me, and I never even knew it—until I looked deeply into my "why."

Your "why" is at the heart of who you are. It is the most important thing you can figure out about yourself and is the reason you do the things you are passionate about. Knowing your "why" allows you to come full circle and be in your personal inspiration zone.

Take a few moments and go back in your mind to a time in your life that was a nexus point. Think about something that happened to you that dramatically changed the direction you were going or that had such a fundamental impact on who you were that it influenced the person you are today. That story is your "why." It may be something big that happened in your life, or it may be something small that had a big impact. Either way, you'll know it if you go back far enough and think about important moments that you had with people that changed your life.

We've all had people who are in "our story." When we talk about how our life has changed through our experiences with them, they are part of that story. However, there is something even more important: The real question is not who's in your story but whose story are you in? Whose life have you made a difference in? That's what creates a meaningful life for yourself and for others.

Next, let's meet Sally Huss, who is over eighty and a former Wimbledon finalist. Sally has written over 100 children's books, and I've had the honor of collaborating on three of them. She is one of my all-time favorite people.

## Sally Huss—Over Eighty and Extremely Balanced

"Do you know what your Achilles' heel is?" the doctor asked as he twirled the gold acupuncture needle in my arm. "No," I said. I didn't know I had one.

I ended up in this particular doctor's office at the insistence of my dance therapy instructor. She knew I was in trouble, but I hardly noticed that there was anything wrong or that I was near death. That's the kind of non-self-awareness an anorexic person has.

"Extremism!" he continued. "In everything you do, you do too much." Well, I could see that, now that he pointed it out. There had been tennis, tennis, tennis when I was young and raised to be a champion. Then there were men, men, men when I discovered the opposite sex. After that, there was squash, squash, squash that I ate imagining it to be the perfect diet for the perfect figure. And, if a little olive oil was good for the liver, I figured a quart must be better. Then, too, if fifteen minutes of meditation were good, certainly a whole day in an out-of-body state would be better!

"Try balance," he suggested. Off I went with a new goal: *balance*. I wrote about it in my notebook; I prayed for it; I looked at the word and tried to absorb it by osmosis. I repeated my new mantra over and over: I am strong. I am capable. *I am balanced!*

Along my path to discover this new state, I learned about change: the simplest way to create it and maintain it. Some information came from books, but more from the wise people who had saved me from myself.

The first thing I learned to do was plant the seed of what I wanted. I planted it deep within me—in cement! *I am balanced!* Then I lived as if I were already in that state. I ate balanced meals. I exercised, but not to exhaustion. I meditated briefly each day. I slept eight hours each night. I felt good because I had already reached my desired state—in my heart. The fruition of this idea would take care of itself, and it did.

Once in a more balanced condition, I began to rewrite my life. I used the same formula to attract the love of my life and create a family. I simply imagined the perfect life partner, held him in my heart before I ever met him, got ready—and one day, on a tennis court in Beverly Hills, he showed up.

I had planted the seed and life delivered the goods—and more. As former head of advertising and promotion for Hallmark Cards, Marv took my artistic talents (I had graduated from USC in fine art) and turned them into a fulfilling art career, developing twenty-six Sally Huss Galleries across the country. These galleries, or happy stores, offered bright images that danced across serigraphs, monoprints, and originals for adults and children. Licensing design work became an extension of the galleries: clothing, ceramics, greeting cards, purses and totes, and more. Writing accompanied some of the small art—little life thoughts to brighten someone's day. Those thoughts turned into a King Features syndicated newspaper panel that ran for twelve years. And so it went until 9/11, when retail everywhere was shut down, including our galleries.

Change again! With no income, the big home in La Jolla went, as did the condo in La Quinta. A friend invited us, apparently homeless, to stay in a small cottage on his art ranch in Fallbrook. It was there that I was guided to do my real work—children's books. I imagined shelves of these books and then put in the effort to create them. These were happy stories in which I could plant a valuable seed in a child— the importance of kindness, the necessity of a good attitude, understanding consequences, and the power of words. In addition, self-worth, self-confidence, learning how to handle fear, good manners, mindfulness and gratitude for the food we are given, and many other topics were touched on and hidden amid amusing rhymes and colorful characters. This catalog of books now numbers over 100 and is still growing.

Where did this drive come from originally? My father. He planted the seed of a champion within me. I was ten when he asked me, "How good do you want to be at tennis?" I had no idea. Then he said, "Why not be a champion?" I thought a moment, and then answered, "Okay."

The seed was planted, and I did the work, later becoming Wimbledon and U.S. Junior Champion, a semifinalist in women's at Wimbledon in singles and doubles. Later I realized the truth: Anyone can be a champion—not necessarily on a scoreboard somewhere, but a champion of himself or herself. Plant the seed of what you want to be or change or develop in your life, hold the image in your heart, then do the work necessary. Nobody can do it for you. Remember, life is wonderful! Don't forget it.

And me? I am a happy person. The happier I am, the happier I get.

● ● ●

I'm so inspired by Ivan and Sally. What did you learn from them? They both remind me daily that we all help one another. Our actions compound.

In Exercises 17 and 18, we are going to discover your personal mastery style and talk about who might benefit from you. Both exercises take a deeper look into how you can take what you know, if you choose to share it with the world.

## POINTS TO PONDER

**Think. Write. Talk. Action.** *(Because practice makes us our best.)*

### EXERCISE 17: Your Mastery Style

Take as long as you need to think about and answer these questions.

1. Would you like to collaborate with someone? Who?

_____

2. Do you have a book to write? What would it be?

_____

3. Would you rather be speaking in front of a crowd of five, twenty-five, 500, 10,000, or not at all? Why?

_____

4. Have people learned from you previously? How?

_____

5. Would you prefer to share a story about another person or share a story about yourself? Why?

_____

6. Would you prefer to be interviewed or give a speech? Why?

_____

7. Would you rather talk with another person in person or on the phone or video? Why?

_____

8. Would you like to mentor another person? Why or why not?

_____

9. If you want to be a mentor, would you like to mentor someone younger than you, the same age as you, or older than you? Why?

_____

10. What other observations do you have about your mastery style?

_____

## EXERCISE 18: All Together Now

Write a few sentences of your life story as if someone else is reporting it.

_____

_____

_____

_____

_____

_____

_____

_____

**Write your personal power statement:**

I am _____.

I specialize in _____.

1. **Who would you share or teach your skill to, or who would listen to your story?**

_____

2. **Who benefits from you?**

_____

3. **Whose life changes because they heard your story and you shared your skill?**

_____

# CHAPTER 10
# IMPACT

*In the point of impact, we become mentors and teachers, using our knowledge to help others and being the change we wish to see in the world. We are leaders who recognize the intangibles. We also recognize that while we are teaching, we are also receptive to being taught. We are lifelong learners. There is respect for others who know a subject better than we do, and we realize there is plenty of room for others. Our impact, comments, and interactions are respectful to all we encounter, even if we challenge the status quo.*

**Can one person really change the world?** The short answer is *yes*! One person really can change the world. How is probably the bigger topic.

## SUCCESS TIP #35: Yes, You Can Change the World; It Starts with You

In our tenth point of change, impact, we may become a mentor or a teacher using our knowledge to help others. Not everyone chooses this path of affecting numbers of people. If you are focused more on individual change, at this moment you can be that change you wish to see in the world. Help make the world a better place. As you do either or both, remember that many will have a lasting impression on your mind. Seek those who have a lasting impression on your soul. Impact is yourself now taking action.

As we change ourselves, we change each other, and we change the world. We are communicators. We are leaders who have learned to recognize the intangibles. We also recognize that while we are teaching, we are receptive to being taught. We are lifelong learners. We have respect for others who know a subject better than we do and allow plenty of room for others. Our impact, comments, and interactions are respectful to all we encounter, even if we challenge the status quo.

You—we—have the possibility in each moment to impact one another in brilliant ways that propel ideas and foster peace, joy, love, and compassion. You now use some of your energy to help others.

The topic of peace is so enormous that many of us are probably left feeling like we need a PhD or two or three, spiritual guru status, or perhaps even a world leader's title to approach the topic. Maybe, maybe not. The more you know, the more open you become to the ideas of others.

Some days all I can think about is peace. I think, *If I could just get each person to see peace, conduct themselves with peace, be tolerant, and so forth—whether it's inner peace, world peace, tolerance, civility, human kindness, or awareness of any version, meaning, or view of the word "peace."* I feel like our world needs a new discussion about care and compassion for ourselves and others.

We are each messengers. We are all capable. Peace in any form starts with each of us. Peace is a me-and-you practice first, which then percolates. It's hard to feel peace—or like we are operating daily to create massive or even tiny drops of social shifts—when some mornings, for example, we don't wake up feeling grateful, happy, worthy, loved, and so on.

Many of us feel the responsibility rests with someone else—that no matter what we do, it might not be enough. Others might feel like each minute they spend here should be dedicated to helping the larger picture. The questions are hard right now and many are entrenched in politics or social issues that can feel too consuming to tackle. I often feel that way, too. The closer one comes to have taken away something they value, the more willing they are to listen and implement change.

To begin, ask yourself a few questions:

- Are you living your daily life with as much well-being, peace, and purpose as you can?
- Are you being your Best Ever You?
- What's your why?
- What's your passion?
- How are you impacting others?

Keep asking questions. Make them up for yourself. Those are just a few that I use. *You may not have solid answers, which is okay.*

Many of us get saddened and perhaps even disgusted when we see things on the news like violence, situations that don't seem fair, unrest, people living in conditions that many of us can't fathom, and more. How much better would we feel with a media diet of stories about awesome achievements, cause-focused assistance, and reports that fill us with joy and happiness. However, our hearts often pour out to those who are sick, hurt, sad, disrupted, and injured for no apparent, comprehensible reason. Wars are going on in places we need to look up, or perhaps in school we learned different names for those now new or separated countries. We may be scratching our heads just simply wondering, *Why?* Since I was a little child, I've felt sensitive and concerned when I see these various situations and have often piped up for various causes, sometimes often just hoping, wishing, and praying someone's life would change for the better.

It's up to us individually to bring to the surface these callings for change or help or cries for love, even if they are just faint murmurs in your heart, soul, and mind. You may not have any real solid reason why you feel this way and you may feel like it is or was a job only a world-famous person could possibly tackle, but the responsibility rests in our own heart, soul, mind, and surface first. While these folks and anyone else you want to add may be much more visible and their messages much more widely known, peace in all forms is up to us each individually first.

When your heart, soul, mind, and surface speak to you, in whispers or shouts or regular voices, are you listening?

Are you giving your wisdom any credibility?

Are you ignoring your instincts, or are you acting on them with meaning and purpose?

How do you feel?

Are you aware that often it is an idea from someone outside the problem? Sometimes problem solving from the outside with one with a clear picture of the whole problem is needed.

It's up to each one of us individually to behave in accordance with basic human standards, and yes, I feel that is a massive, much larger topic. You can call it civility, human dignity, human rights, and more. I know that it makes my head, heart, soul, spirit, surface, and energy spin and whole being just cringe when I see wrongdoing. I'm not sure I know what all those standards are precisely, but we as individuals know if our heart, mind, soul, and surface feel they are even slightly violated in any way. You most likely know what you will and will not tolerate, and we all know when we have those feelings of wrong versus right and even the murky shades of change in between. Sometimes the question "How?" enters the picture at about this time. One idea is to raise your children to care and be involved. The pebble you throw in the water casts a wide wave.

You may have just had a fight with your spouse or dislike your own neighbor or even family members. Perhaps you haven't felt well this past week and you are behind in your schoolwork or other work. Your jaw may be dropping at what you just saw on television. You may feel some personal violation or unjust situation. You may feel like the percolator is unplugged and not brewing up your boldest blend. I get it. I want to use the word "despite" here to remind us that despite what is going on, at the heart of us is love and compassion. We may have lost sight of love and compassion personally, professionally, or otherwise, and it's up to us to bring these back to ourselves so we can percolate them to others.

Think with your heart. It's pausing for a moment to think about another human being. Perhaps it's pausing to think about your own behavior. What comes from your heart, soul, mind, spirit, and surface? It's sharing your light and love with yourself and others. It's your peaceful intentions and acts that emanate into the world. It is by helping others that we find peace and joy. Are you teaching love, compassion, and morality by your example?

What do you do to help others? Are you embracing your space, time, and energy to your highest percolating potential? Do you feel like you are loved and bring compassion and understanding to yourself and others around you?

I was recently at the grocery store in the pet food aisle. There was an older woman on the floor basically crouched on her knees picking out cans of cat food. I was next to her picking out cat food as well but had more of a bent-at-the-waist form. She said, "You are lucky you can bend like that. I'm so old I can't do that at all. It hurts my back." I smiled and said, "You are lucky you can be on your knees because my old gymnastic knees can't take that." We both laughed and helped each other up. She had instant tears in her eyes. Crying she said, "You know, aging can be really hard. I lost my husband four years ago and things just aren't the same. I used to do this with him and since then no one has even helped me when I've been stuck on the floor in pain in this aisle. It usually takes me a lot longer to get back up."

We each had such tender souls and loving energy toward each other. We chatted so long our feet began to hurt. I ended up giving her my phone number to call me, especially over the winter, if she needed help because her family doesn't live close. On my way out, I saw her in another line waiting, so as I was exiting, I also asked a young man to assist her to her car, which he so very kindly did.

I share this story with you not because of what I did but rather to ask you to stop and pause when you encounter other human beings. Look around. You meet people in your life for a reason that might just not be clear to you at the time. Even in this day and age of everything being so fast paced, many people are slowed down and in need of assistance. Your interactions with each person you encounter matter.

Your call may be more state-focused, national, or worldwide than a local chance meeting at a grocery store. We all can do what we can. From the door you open to the smile you share to some other act of kindness, these moments matter to you and others. Someone might need some cash in their pocket and never show it. If you have it, give it.

Peace in any shape or form starts with me and you and becomes us and we.

As I sit here on this glorious Maine June day with it gently raining and the wind rushing through the trees, our feeders filled with colorful birds and one of the cats sitting beside me, it is so peaceful, and I am reminded once again that I am lucky. My life hasn't been super peaceful all the time and I've definitely needed support over the years.

I've mentioned throughout the book that I have life-threatening food allergies, called anaphylaxis. I live my daily life allergic to peanuts, tree nuts, fish, and shellfish. I developed these allergies in my late twenties. I'm grateful to our food allergy community and, in particular, Eleanor Garrow-Holding and everyone at the Food Allergy Anaphylaxis Connection Team (FAACT) for their support over the years. When I was first diagnosed with food allergies back in 1998, it was so terrible to navigate as it was unclear what foods I was allergic to. I even had an allergic reaction to the allergy tests! Now that I know what foods exactly, I am able to live my life more fully. My life was less than peaceful when the emergency room doctor saved my life back in 1998 from one of my worst allergic reactions. That moment has had a forever impact on my life. Then again in 1999 when I had the worst allergic reaction of my life while six months' pregnant with our son Cam, the word "lucky" was used, only this time for the both of us. I've had multiple instances over the last twenty years when my husband, Peter, has had to take emergency measures to save my life.

Please understand, you don't need to feel lucky or have your life endangered or have an illness to—in this moment—stop, pivot, and change. You hold your power, you hold your moments, and you are the driver of change if you choose to be. Today really is the beginning of the rest of your life.

This brings us to the topic of random acts of kindness.

## SUCCESS TIP #36: Amplify Your Positive Impact

Talk about amplifying your positive impact! In our house, all of our kids were raised doing random acts of kindness. They each will tell you they have a moment in their childhood when they remember an act of kindness or a few that we did. Our youngest went on a business trip with us to Washington, D.C. No trip to D.C. is complete, to us, without visiting our favorite bagel shop. We went in, stood in line, and when it was our turn, we quietly said we wanted to pay for the four people after us. Quaid just thought that was the coolest thing ever. That moment stuck with him. In his last year of high school, he and I created the Percolate Project for his senior project. Almost every state has now participated, of course, with much more to do. The concept is to randomly pay for someone's coffee or order in back of you and pass along the orange Percolate Project card. We've had a person even pay off another's medical bills. Don't expect accolades, praise, and thank-you moments coming your way when you do this. These are anonymous. I do, however, believe that if you are the recipient of a random act of kindness, give the universe a giant *thank-you* and pay it forward when you can. My mom and I were in line in a coffee shop the day after my father died, and we were handed a piece of paper. Our order had been paid for. We couldn't believe the timing of the universe!

## SUCCESS TIP #37: There Are Two Words You Can Never Overuse: "Thank You."

Through our son Quaid and our community here in Maine, I've come to meet Haley Stark. Her story really resonates with me. From my experiences with my dad, I understand how recovery from a stroke of any kind can be. I have a place near and dear in my heart for stroke survival and stroke awareness. When I think of this, I don't think of teenagers going through what Haley has endured. Both Haley and Quaid are honors graduates of Falmouth High School in Falmouth, Maine. Haley now attends Harvard. Please meet Haley Stark as she tells us about a change she certainly didn't choose and the multiple unforeseen circumstances she faced.

## Stories from the Heart
### Haley Stark—Surviving Trauma

In life, embracing heartache can be as necessary as promoting positivity. While sharing stories about overcoming challenges that test their spirit, trauma survivors can exclude the unprepossessing details—those constituting hair loss, mental or physical breakdowns, self-doubt and self-degradation, or even thoughts or actions of self-harm. Why wouldn't they? Certainly, these overcomers are entitled to minorly embellish the accounts of their journeys to satisfy the psychological, human need to dull memories of extreme grief and frustration. However, exclusion of severe pain and sadness from retellings can paint unrealistic and unattainable portraits of resilience for audiences; it can blur the human experience by focusing too sharply on goodness and achievement.

When we produce content for our social media accounts and share our experiences with the tier of friends, family, and acquaintances too unfamiliar with us to discover our "true" selves, we intentionally obscure reality. We edit, crop out, and delete thousands of photos before selecting the one that masks our insecurities and generates a faultless representation of our being. We obsessively track responses, likes, and praise. As a nineteen-year-old, I have only ever lived in a universe with two worlds: the physical and digital. Throughout the entirety of my life, I have fashioned and maintained a persona for our illusory existence in the virtual realm—the construct of a woman who, quite frankly, I hardly resemble in actuality.

I do not fancy myself any sort of public figure, but when my community was following live updates of my recovery, I felt a pressure to perform. With love letters and "get well soon" balloons flooding my hospital's mailbox, I felt I had to seem effortlessly motivated, stubbornly concentrated on conquering, and basically invincible—to relieve them of their secondhand stress and worry. Now I feel a pressure to revisit my story with authenticity.

Authenticity is not solely derived from sadness and pain; the uplifting chapters of my story are sometimes comparably as sincere. My concern is the balance, or lack thereof, of "sadness" and "happiness" that we choose to present to others. If we started appreciating and welcoming the discomfort of listening to stories of despair, we may find a worldwide community of people who willingly hide their pain for the sake of an image. We constantly absorb a chimera created by social media that subconsciously distorts our vision in the so-called real world when we confuse it with physical reality. If discussion of the pain and imperfection that the digital, social sphere rejects was normalized, we could alleviate society from the imaginary sense of uniqueness, the loneliness, and the isolation felt when one endures pain.

Pain and loss are part of evolving and growing, yet pain and loss are disbarred from one of the worlds in which we modernly live. We ought to perceive social media posts, including our own, as tabloids—entertainment, theatrics, not reality. Similarly, we ought to approach others' stories with critical thinking. Internalizing toxic positivity, hearing only the good, while ignoring suffering can be as detrimental to our well-being as exclusively consuming stories of loss and sorrow.

Authenticity has grounded me after years of trying to conform to an ideal candidate for college applications: someone who faces adversity head-on, rarely struggles, and overcomes obstacles with an evolved point of view and strength, not with any lasting heartbreak, uncertainty, or depression that could hinder future success. I thought that in order to achieve greatness, I had to keep propelling this façade forward. Luckily, I dialed back on this mission before I lost the distinction between the character and myself. The genuine version of me has not yet fully recovered from her trauma.

At twelve, I suffered a rare spinal cord stroke that left me entirely immobile and unfeeling yet still cognitively intact. While lying in the coffinlike chamber of a five-hour MRI, I vividly recall evaluating my future. In the natural order of adolescent priority, I wondered if I would return home in time for school the next morning. Frantic doctors strung my unmoving limbs through countless inconclusive examinations: a spinal tap, angiogram, CT scan, and three MRIs would diagnose me with a stroke a neurologist claimed he had never encountered and hoped to never encounter again.

An exceptional pain struck my right shoulder just hours after routine track practice. I reported the symptoms to my father, who promptly administered Tylenol. While adjusting myself restlessly on our living room sofa, the sharp sensation rapidly spread across my body. For a fleeting moment, all my muscles tightened and trapped me in utter agony. Then, ninety seconds passed, and a release overwhelmed me. I was completely paralyzed.

Baffled doctors revealed to my parents that I would be forever paralyzed, unable to breathe on my own. They recommended the immediate and permanent attachment of a ventilator. In a defiant, desperate attempt to save my life, I was transferred to a Boston hospital. Throughout the transfer, I contracted pneumonia, sepsis, and eventually septic shock. My deteriorating conditions rendered my survival nothing short of miraculous.

My hunger was satisfied by the dispensing of a glucose and water concoction through feeding tubes. Excruciating sensations pierced my shoulder, ironically indicating the onset of recovery. Recovery would be accompanied by discouraging setbacks, mental torment, and a major dependency on nurses. Regardless of the circumstances, I chose to maintain a positive outlook.

I was graciously blanketed with optimism from my community. I began inpatient rehabilitation after eleven days in intensive care. I ritualistically engaged in physical, occupational, and speech therapies for nearly fifty days of rehab. Despite medical odds, I reclaimed the ability to breathe, eat, and talk without assistance.

I escaped the confines of my hospital bed and eventually the limits of a wheelchair. At the end of my inpatient stay at Spaulding Rehabilitation Hospital, I limped beyond the entrance with a walker. Even with substantial weakness on my right side requiring years of outpatient therapy, I relished my triumph.

My residual deficits include minor sensation weakness on my right side and the inability to move my right hand. The remaining physical damage from my stroke is nonetheless incomparable to the fortune and privilege I have obtained. I have been given insight into the strength of humanity. Particularly, I have witnessed raw, uncensored battles between life-threatening illness and innocent children; I have witnessed courage in its truest form. After my battle, I feel wholeheartedly responsible to use my recovered being as a vessel to serve the families on the pediatric floors of my hospitals. I published a memoir recounting the stages of my stroke titled *Tying the Ribbon: How I Survived a Spinal Cord Stroke at Twelve Years Old—and My Life Afterward* and have donated the proceeds. I have worked tirelessly to transform societal discomfort with disabilities through writing and public speaking. Ultimately, I have overcome. Overcoming and recovering do not necessarily sync.

I am unfamiliar with the young athlete I was before my injury, yet I yearn for a chance to talk to her. Upon greeting her, I would extend a lifeless hand. Sensitive to how little time she has with her health, I would speak unhesitatingly. I would prepare her briefly, gently, withholding the impending pain and uncertainty.

Then, after reveling in her potential, I'd demand she sprint away from me.

I would watch as she hurries from our conversation. Although her fear may leave her breathless, she does not suffocate; she will conquer great strides in denser air. She will clear tremendous hurdles and fill bleachers with spectators who will cherish her victories. She is young and unknowing now, but I am the living proof that she will find her way.

I overcame my physical injury as best as I could, but rising above the mental toll my stroke took on me is a lifelong undertaking. Instead of feeling like I need immediate answers or results, or that I need to appear like some untouchable victor, I feel excited for the lifetime of energy I will pour into my development and take advantage of my past for my evolution.

I'm not trying to advise you to spend the rest of your time thinking and talking about sadness. I just want you to accept the ever-persistent presence of pain in every individual's life. Celebrate that you are a sentient human capable of feeling and experiencing a perhaps infinite spectrum of emotions. Life, in all its glory and hurt, is remarkable. Stop submitting to perfectionism and discerning social media's idea of perfection as a reasonable standard for yourself. You are worthy of *every* version of yourself.

I implore you to appreciate the convergence of two opposing forces, good and evil, which complicate yet enrich every single thing you experience. Allow yourself to approach your self-actualization with not only a tolerance for your flaws but an admiration of them. Remember your mistakes as clearly as you remember your greatest accomplishments. Let go of trying to expend painful human emotion to appear to yourself or others as something ultimately inhuman, something *superhuman*.

For several years of my life, I repelled therapy, reflection, and self-care in a bid to create an impressive version of me on paper or in speeches: the version that naturally converted life-altering trauma into a well-contained, inspiring, and motivating story of triumph. Every once in a while, people need bursts of inspiration and want to hear only the good. Furthermore, I do perceive my physical progress as a triumph, yet I also see it as miraculous, considering the mental and physical torment associated with full-body paralyzation (albeit somewhat temporary). It has taken until now for me to understand that writing a book, giving speeches, getting into Harvard, and feeling accomplished does not guarantee a sense of feeling whole. Wholeness comes from reminding yourself of the entire story, regardless of your audience. The other elements of my personal, human experience: the depression I underplayed and the struggle I refused to admit to battling since the day of my injury onward are also as key to my growth as my luck, blessings, and ability to cling to positivity when it counts. Books, speeches, and narratives take into account an audience, just as social media posts do for the average member of society nowadays. Therefore, you must disassociate from your audience in your quiet self-reflection, and occasionally give yourself the pleasure of hearing your genuine, authentic, unabridged, and unrevised story.

You are complicated. You will complete your life one day with some ratio of suffering to joy, and even though I hope your balance leans in the direction of your happiness, I also hope you welcome the complexities of the human condition and find beauty in, or at least have a fascination with, *all* the good and the bad of everything you endure.

● ● ●

Haley also appeared on our radio show as a guest on December 8, 2019, to discuss her book, *Tying the Ribbon*.

Haley's story reminds us that sometimes change and circumstances are not of our choosing, yet we are given the choice to move forward and have the ability to choose our path. We may need support from others in order to do so. Our next story reminds us of our abilities and resilience as well.

My honor is to present to you a story from the Honorable Olympia J. Snowe, a trailblazer senator whose leadership organization sends ripples of positive change throughout the universe.

### Senator Olympia J. Snowe—Making an Impact

I was born in Augusta, Maine, in 1947 and spent my early childhood living in Lewiston with my hardworking parents—my father a Greek immigrant and my mother a first-generation American. My mother passed away when I was eight, and I lost my father, too, less than a year later. By the time I was orphaned at age nine, I was already attending St. Basil Academy—a girls' school founded by the Greek Orthodox Church in New York.

After six years I decided to move back to Auburn, Maine, and live with my aunt and uncle's family. I went to Edward Little High School and then the University of Maine, where I majored in political science.

From my early years I had an innate interest in government, specifically in the way of helping others. After losing both of my parents at such a young age, I had tremendous empathy for people who work hard and, through no fault of their own, have terrible things happen in their lives and need support to get on their feet again. I naturally gravitated toward political positions in my early twenties.

In 1973 at age twenty-six, I was working for Congressman Bill Cohen (who later served as a U.S. senator and then secretary of defense) when my first husband was killed in an auto accident on the way home from the Maine State Legislature. I was devastated. That said, my early experience with loss informed my reaction. I had found that the best way to manage grief was to keep moving forward and make the best of a negative situation. I was encouraged by colleagues, friends, and family to run in a special election to fill his seat in the Maine House of Representatives, and I won.

Though the circumstances were far from ideal for undertaking an election, I felt extremely fortunate for the opportunity to dive into new work and pursue a career I was passionate about. Ultimately, that path took me through the Maine State Senate, the U.S. House, and the U.S. Senate as well—with some incredible milestones along the way. When first elected to the U.S. House in 1978, I was the youngest Republican woman and first Greek American woman ever elected to Congress. I also served as First Lady of Maine for five years after marrying my former colleague in the U.S. House and then governor of Maine, John McKernan.

After my election to the U.S. Senate in 1994, I also became the first woman in American history to serve in both houses of a state legislature and both houses of Congress. And throughout my career, I endeavored to lead with an approach that valued a thorough studying of the issues, listening to and respecting the viewpoints of others, and building consensus to find solutions.

When I decided not to seek reelection to the Senate in 2012 due to the excessive polarization in Congress, I wanted to continue making a difference for others. My priority became finding a new way to give back to my state and lift up the next generation of Maine women.

Forty years of public service taught me just how critical it is to have women with strong ideas and voices at the table—assuming prominent roles in problem solving and leading their communities.

After researching the challenges confronting young women today, I founded the Olympia Snowe Women's Leadership Institute. I was struck by the distressing statistics that girls lose confidence and self-esteem at alarming rates as they transition from middle to high school. The institute was born from a desire to reverse those trends and address the decreasing confidence levels of Maine girls—to give young women the tools and mentorship needed to overcome obstacles and realize their full potential.

The institute is designed to help girls in the program—known as Olympia's Leaders, or OLs—build the skills required to be leaders in their lives, families, careers, and communities. Our three-year curriculum is delivered in the tenth, eleventh, and twelfth grades by trained female volunteers like Elizabeth—known as Olympia's Leaders Advisors, or OLAs.

Each year begins with an intensive one-day kickoff session called the Fall Forum, in which all the OLs hear from me and other accomplished women, followed by monthly meetings with their OLAs. During their sophomore year, OLs identify their values, strengths, and passions. Then, as juniors, girls leverage their self-knowledge to choose what messages they want to share, learn how best to articulate them, and practice how to listen and respond to others' ideas. Finally, during their senior year, they map visions for their future and learn how to adapt their plans and mind-sets in case they decide to change course.

My institute is having a significant impact on hundreds of young lives, and I am deeply grateful to be able to use my own life story to inspire these future women leaders. We all possess a boundless capacity for achievement, but the line between our aspirations and their realization is never a straight one. The program teaches girls that they inevitably will be presented with obstacles and roadblocks in their lives—but what matters is how they confront those challenges. It is always possible to distill triumph from adversity. I am living proof of that!

● ● ●

Thank you to Senator Olympia J. Snowe for sharing her inspirational and inspiring story. I'm certain some of the choices she made were not easy. We're glad she made them and bravely found a beautiful future. The women in Maine are blessed to have a strong, caring, and impactful leader to guide them. Knowing her story, when I think of the Honorable Olympia J. Snowe, I think of the word "brave." Working with the young women through the Olympia Snowe Leadership Institute certainly has taught me more about bravery.

Remember to help others be brave. Do what you can do. Your smile may change a life. It could be your time. It could be a moment. You always have the power to help out another person in ways that take only a bit of your energy.

Exercises 19 and 20 examine changing lives and impacting others. Think about turning your change or your unforeseen circumstance into something from which people can learn. We learn by sharing our stories, and we also learn with community.

## POINTS TO PONDER

**Think. Write. Talk. Action.** *(Because practice makes us our best.)*

### EXERCISE 19: Change a Life

1. What is a change you made or an unforeseen circumstance you have been adjusting to?

_____

2. If you were to take one step today to create your positive impact on others, what is that?

_____

• Find one person online as a resource.
• Find one person in person as a resource.

### EXERCISE 20: Your Impact—Your Leadership

Reach out to the people in Exercise 19 and offer your assistance in helping others. Next, while you are waiting for a response, think about this: What small change did you, as one person make, that ultimately may change another person's life and impact them positively?

_____

_____

1. Do you have larger plans?

_____

_____

2. What are those plans?

_____

_____

## SUCCESS TIP #38: Finish Strong!

So here we are together at the end of this book, which feels like a new beginning to me and I hope to you as well. I'd really like to remind you also of serendipity and coincidence. Things may happen for a reason. You may be the recipient of great, unexpected luck. These are all wonderful forms of success. They can result in success that can't be conventionally measured.

## SUCCESS TIP #39: Remember to Look for the Extraordinary in the Everyday and Ordinary

Marvelous moments are everywhere. Create and practice pausing and create and embrace space to slow down to appreciate all the moments in your life. You now have the tools in your toolbox from reading this book and completing these exercises to become and maintain your authentic Best Ever You.

## SUCCESS TIP #40: Create a Vision and Practice That Vision and Really Live Where Each Moment in Your Life Matters

Connect with your true self, to others around you, and to the world as a whole in peace and for peace. Embrace your inner love, gifts, and talents that are the essence of who you are and share your uniqueness with the world.

Enjoy everyday miracles. They are there. They are success from our hearts.

Your heart matters.

Your truths matter.

Your energy matters.

You matter.

Love to you all, and thank you so much for being with me.

—Elizabeth

## DISCUSSION AND OPTIONAL MASTER CLASS CERTIFICATION

For those who wish to obtain our *Change Guidebook* master class certification, please submit your answers on the website here: besteveryou.com/changeguidebook.

For those wishing to just continue and enjoy learning about change, these discussion questions are here for you to complete at your own pace for fun and learning reinforcement. These questions also make wonderful book club discussion points.

1. Please write a valuable lesson or two that you learned from Part 1: "Align Your Heart."

2. What are the Ten Points of Change?

3. What is the purpose of the Ten Points of Change?

4. What is one of your "incredible yes" moments in your life?

5. What are the six questions you can ask yourself when presented with a choice or decision that needs to be made? Which question resonates with you the most?

6. What is a vision statement and why is it so powerful?

7. What is a valuable lesson you learned from Part 2: "Align Your Truths?"

8. Which two stories from the book were your favorite and why?

9. What does MAP stand for?

_____

10. What are two of your goals?

_____

11. What is your viewpoint on change?

_____

12. What is Elizabeth's spaghetti theory?

_____

13. Would you rather have $1 million or 1 million hours? Why?

_____

14. Do you consider yourself a patient person? Why or why not?

_____

15. Please write a valuable lesson you learned from Part 3: "Align Your Energy."

_____

16. What is one skill or piece of knowledge you have, and who do you think can benefit from it and why?

_____

17. How can you, as one person, have an impact on humanity?

_____

18. Have you ever received or given a random act of kindness? What was it?

_____

19. Who has helped you in your life? How?

20. How has this book impacted your life?

**Congratulations! You did it!**

# ABOUT THE AUTHOR

**Elizabeth Hamilton-Guarino** is a bestselling author of multiple books in the self-help and children's book genres, including the bestseller *PERCOLATE: Let Your Best Self Filter Through* and the award-winning Pinky Doodle Bug children's book series. She is a personal and professional development consultant and Certified Master Coach, who certifies others to become Professional Life Coaches.

As the founder of the Best Ever You Network and chief executive officer of Compliance4, Elizabeth has helped thousands around the globe be their best and achieve world-class excellence. As a trusted leader, speaker, and author, Elizabeth provides development and training to individuals and organizations around the world. Elizabeth also consults with companies regarding their branding efforts, to establish a positive online presence, engage their clients, and position the company and develop their brand appropriately and ethically in social media. An expert in mentoring people to market their strengths and achieve brand excellence, she works with clients worldwide to illuminate their light within, develop their best life, and become their Best Ever You with gratitude-based behavior and belief systems. Guarino is the creator and host of the long-standing radio show

*The Best Ever You Show*, which has millions of downloads and live listens and is syndicated.

Elizabeth lives her daily life with multiple life-threatening food allergies. Elizabeth serves as a spokesperson for the Food Allergy and Anaphylaxis Connection Team (FAACT) and MedicAlert Foundation and works tirelessly to help all with food allergies stay alive and thrive. Elizabeth and Sally Huss teamed up to create the best-selling children's books *A Lesson for Every Child: Learning About Food Allergies, Self-Confident Sandy*, and *Best Ever You*. Guarino was also featured in the book *One of the Gang* with football great Jerome Bettis.

Elizabeth is a member of the Forbes Business Council and serves as a Leadership Advisor for the Olympia Snowe Women's Leadership Institute and serves as youth advisor and mentor to young women in high school in the state of Maine. She was appointed to and serves on the Town of Falmouth, Maine's Wellness Committee.

Elizabeth and her husband, Peter, donate time, money, and more to enrich the lives of others and support good causes. She has baked and donated tens of thousands of chocolate chip cookies for organizations throughout the United States in connection with children's literacy and youth sports. Her cookies have won first place at the Cumberland Fair in Maine.

Elizabeth and Peter have four sons, three rescued cats, and two Bernedoodles. They live in Falmouth, Maine. They can be found in their garden, in the pool, raking leaves, or shoveling snow, depending on the season, the way life should be.

Elizabeth's hashtags—#BestEverYou, #TipstoBeYourBest, and #TheChangeGuidebook—are widely circulated. Visit besteveryou.com/changeguidebook for more information.